And Still We Rise

An Introduction to Black Liberation Theology

Diana L. Hayes, Ph.D., S.T.D.

For Delores
God bless!
Diana Hayes

PAULIST PRESS
New York and Mahwah, N.J.

also by Diana L. Hayes
published by Paulist Press

HAGAR'S DAUGHTERS: WOMANIST
WAYS OF BEING IN THE WORLD

Cover design by Cynthia Dunne.
Cover art courtesy of Springer/Bettmann Film Archive.

The Publisher gratefully acknowledges use of the following selection:
excerpts from "And Still I Rise," by Maya Angelou, Copyright © 1978
by Maya Angelou. Reprinted by permission of Random House, Inc.

Library of Congress Cataloging-in-Publication Data

Hayes, Diana L.
    And still we rise : an introduction to Black liberation theology /
Diana L. Hayes.
        p.   cm.
    Includes bibliographical references and index.
    ISBN 0-8091-3622-8 (alk. paper)
    1. Black theology. 2. Liberation theology. 3. Afro-Americans—
Religion. 4. Afro-Americans—Social conditions. I. Title.
BT82.7.H38   1996   95-20728
230'.089'96—dc20   CIP

Published by Paulist Press
997 Macarthur Boulevard
Mahwah, New Jersey 07430

Printed and bound in the
United States of America

Contents

iii

For the generations of African Americans who continue
"to rise".

You may write me down in history
With your bitter, twisted lies,
You may trod me in the very dirt
But still, like dust, I'll rise....

Out of the huts of history's shame
I rise
Up from a past that's rooted in pain
I rise
I'm a black ocean, leaping and wide,
Welling and swelling I bear in the tide
Leaving behind nights of terror and fear
I rise
Into a daybreak that's wondrously clear
I rise
Bringing the gifts that my ancestors gave,
I am the dream and the hope of the slave.
I rise.
I rise.
I rise.

Maya Angelou, "Still I Rise"

Introduction:
Why a Black
Liberation Theology?

A universal definition of theology has, historically, been that of Anselm: "Theology is faith seeking understanding." If we accept this as a basic premise, then the contemporary efforts of African Americans in the United States, and of people of African ancestry[1] throughout the world, to articulate their faith in a manner and style as well as from within a context that is consistent with their own lived experience should be understood as theology in its most classical understanding.

The history of Black Americans in the United States of America reveals a constant, unending struggle against political, economic, social, and religious forces which have attempted to deny the reality of Black people as human beings. From their earliest presence in this country to the present day, Blacks have had to struggle against the bondage of slavery, oppression, and second-class status. Their culture has been denied, their feelings and humanity have been ignored or belittled, their desires and ambitions thwarted. Yet they have continued to struggle toward a goal which was expressed only in the word "freedom." This was seen to be not merely a spiritual freedom coming only after death, despite the preachings and urgings of white ministers that salvation was the heavenly reward for good slaves, but also a material, physical freedom which could be grasped in the here and now. It was a freedom which would put food of one's own choosing on the table, a roof of one's own choice over one's head, and an education and employment in keeping with one's intelligence and ability within one's reach. This was the freedom sought by most, one still being sought today by many.

It is out of this context, the unending search for an undeniable freedom, that Black Theology developed. It arose in response to the frustrated rage and violence of the Black ghettos of the 1960s, in the muddy marches for voting rights in the South, and in the growing dichotomy between a Christianity which preached love and non-violence to Blacks while it practiced hatred, racism, segregation, and other forms of structural and physical violence against them. However, it must also be recognized that Black Theology existed in a more embryonic form long before this.

The immediate and catalytic origins of Black Theology can be found in three individual but related events: a) the Civil Rights movement in the United States, b) the Black Power movement, which began as a critique of the above movement but quickly developed its own thrust and momentum, and c) the publication, in 1964, of *Black Religion: The Negro and Christianity in the United States*[2] by Joseph Washington.

However, in order to fully understand both the development and the significance of Black Theology for today, it will be necessary to explore not only these movements (Chapter 3) but earlier movements and influences (Chapters 1 and 2) which have taken place during the long history of the Black presence in the United States. In so doing, we will see revealed the continuous interaction of a people with their God as they sought to answer questions such as these: Who is God for African Americans? What is the meaning of the death and resurrection of Jesus Christ for us? What is the meaning and purpose of Black existence in the United States?

These questions called forth a reflective praxis, engaging African Americans in a retrieval of their collective past and a projection into their future in order to resolve what many saw as a conflict between Blackness and Christian faith as well as the role of religion in the struggle for economic, social and physical liberation.

Black Theology developed as a response to this conflict, seeking to answer for Black Americans, especially those whose origins lay in slavery, and others of the African diaspora, the questions of identity and belonging that continued to concern them. Continued reflection on the Black historical experience in the United States has led to further questions: Why is there a need for a Black Theology today? What form(s) should that theology take? What is or was the role and significance of the Black Power movement and Malcolm X in its development? What is or was the impact of Martin Luther King's theology of Christian love and non-violence? What is the role and importance of Black history, culture, and experience in Black Theology?

After Black Theology was more firmly established in the late 1980s, yet another set of questions were raised by those who had not been included in the earlier dialogue. Ironically, Black Theology, a theology of, for, and by the Black oppressed, itself failed to recognize, initially, forms of oppression other than racial oppression. As the number of Black women increased in programs of theological study and roles of pastoral leadership, they began to raise their voices in a critique of the sexism found in the Black Theology movement and to explore the development of a new womanist theology of liberation which seeks to address oppression, whether racial, sexual or economic, in a more holistic and communitarian way.

In addition, other people of color, both within the United States and outside of it, but especially in Latin America, criticized Black Theology for its failure to deal with issues of economic (class) oppression, an issue which has become of increasing importance as the Black middle class has grown, both in numbers and importance, at the same time that an impoverished, ill-educated and seemingly permanent Black underclass has appeared.

Finally, Black Catholics, who were involved to a less prominent degree in the Civil Rights movement but who were active in it, are today beginning to readdress many of the questions raised by Black Theology in its beginnings in the 1960s but from within the perspective of their faith as Roman Catholics. Their perspective is both Black and Catholic; their issues are the same, yet also different; their concerns are increasingly pressing as they re-embrace an African and Christian heritage which has existed for almost two thousand years.

In this introductory survey, we will, therefore, begin by looking at the early history of Blacks in this country, the ties that remained between African American and African cultures and their influence (Chapter 1) as well as the significance of the Great Awakenings of the eighteenth and nineteenth centuries, and the revivals and missions that resulted from them, on what became Black Christianity (Chapter 2). We will then move into a discussion of Black Christianity itself and the beginnings of an articulated systematic theology of liberation (Chapter 3). The sources (African American history, cul-

ture and experience, Christian tradition and Sacred
Scripture) and norm (faith in Jesus Christ) of Black
Theology will then be critically explored (Chapter 4) as
well as the particular methodologies of such theologians
as James Cone, Gayraud Wilmore and J. Deotis Roberts
and the language of symbol and metaphor, narrative and
testimony emerging from the Black historical experience
which grounds their theologizing (Chapters 5 and 6).
Those voices absent in the earlier stages of Black
Theology will also be discussed, especially those of Black
women and Black Catholics in order to provide a broader
perspective of Black Theology as it is articulated today
(Chapters 7 and 8).

Finally, the future of Black Theology will be addressed.
Is there still a need for a Black Theology of liberation and,
if so, what form(s) should that theology take? Who are and
will be the spokespersons for that theology? Will Black
Theology continue to evolve into an academic theology
only or will it be able to re-engage itself in the context
from which it first emerged, that of African Americans
and their journeying with God in the Christian churches
and in this land? If the latter is to occur, how will it be
done? And how will Black Theology continue to impact
upon a nation and a faith struggling with its multicultural
past and its increasingly multicultural future? All of these
questions cannot be answered but an attempt at setting
the dialogue will be made.

James Cone, the first to articulate a specifically Black
Liberation Theology in this century, has stated that "I
firmly believe that the issues to which theology addresses
itself should be those that emerge out of life in society as
persons seek to achieve meaning in a dehumanized
world."[3] Black Theology is an outgrowth of the experience
of being Black and oppressed in the United States. It is a
theology which seeks, first, to speak to all Black people

from within their own context. It seeks to explain what it means to them to be Black and Christian. Only then does it look beyond the Black community and present itself, without apology, to the rest of the Christian world.

This work is a brief, critical introduction to Black Liberation Theology. Although addressed to both a scholarly and a popular audience, it does not attempt to address all of the issues and developments of that theology but rather to introduce readers to the major issues, ideas, concerns and proponents in the field and to provide resources for further, more in-depth, exploration of it.

Notes

1. Throughout this text, I will use the term African American to depict those Black Americans whose origins date from the period of slavery in the United States whether their ancestors were slave or free. The term Black or Black American will be used to designate all peoples of Black African descent and of the African diaspora, wherever they now live, but especially those of the Caribbean, South and Central America, Canada and Mexico, and Africa itself who have, in this century, immigrated to the United States. The term Black American is, therefore, to be seen as a category inclusive of African Americans.

2. Joseph R. Washington, *Black Religion: The Negro and Christianity in the United States* (Lanham, Md.: University Press of America, 1984; originally published New York: Beacon Press, 1966).

3. James H. Cone, *For My People: Black Theology and the Black Church* (Maryknoll, NY: Orbis, 1984), p. 28.

1

African Roots and American Branches

African Americans, throughout their long and often painful history in the United States, have been engaged in a theological quest, the development and articulation of an understanding of God which is both Christian and Black, one which speaks of "who" they are and "whose" they are. It is a theology reflective of the dialectical struggle which is a constant underlying aspect of their reality, a dialectic which creates a tension between the radical action toward freedom on their own terms and a passive acquiescence seen in the acceptance of assimilation.[1]

As we shall see in this brief text, to be Black and Christian in the United States has been, at one and the same time, a comfort and a trial for a people who trace their presence here to the "zeal" of Christian slave traders and missionaries to convert the "pagan" Africans, thereby allegedly saving their souls from hell. The failure to acknowledge the more urgent reasons—that of the economic need for a cheap, plentiful and permanent labor force that was easily identifiable—for Christian participation in a slave trade which, over a period of less than two hundred years, depleted the continent of Africa of many of its ablest and strongest peoples resulted in a proselytization of Blacks which was hypocritical, at the least, and which seriously distorted and denied the true teachings of Christ and the Christian churches, at its worst.[2]

Indoctrinated into a Christianity which upheld their degradation and dehumanization,[3] many of the African slaves rebelled. For some that rebellion took the form of actual physical revolt, fought with whatever weapons came to hand, and was condemned to failure due to the lack of weapons, insufficient numbers or betrayal from within.[4] But rebellion took other forms as well, most especially the refusal to accept a "watered-down" Christianity and an emasculated Christ. The African slaves and their descendants, instead, were able, miraculously in light of their circumstances, to recognize the true being of Christ and his message of a salvific liberation for all humanity. Despite their lack of formal theological training or scholarly knowledge, this enslaved people engaged in their own reflection on Scripture and Christ's message and began to lay the foundations for a Black Theology of Liberation which has been simmering for over three hundred years and which finally came to a turbulent boil, bursting into public awareness in the late 1960s.

Black Liberation Theology is the product of African American peoples, both slave and free, who sought and continue to seek to understand and articulate their faith in God and that faith's persistence over almost four hundred years of slavery, persecution, discrimination and dehumanization. It is their effort to "defend the faith (hope) which is (theirs)" (1 Pet 3:15) and has been theirs for centuries. It is a theology with roots deep in the soil of Africa and branches coming to fruition in the United States, for it speaks of the efforts of a people forcibly and unwillingly torn from their native land and brought to a strange land where, stripped of their humanity and denied the basic dignity promised to all of God's creation, they were, paradoxically, able to survive, grow strong, and evolve into a mighty nation.[5]

African Roots

In order to understand Black Theology, it is necessary to begin where the people whose expression of faith it is themselves began, in Africa. The African peoples, from many nations and language groups, who were brought to this country were a people with a rich and diverse history. Africa is a continent, not one nation; therefore, its peoples come from different cultures and traditions. Their languages, manner of dress, living styles, social habits, and religious beliefs vary, but all provided a source and way of life that, far from being "brutal, nasty and short," was religiously based, community oriented, socially-sustaining and economically viable.[6]

> Traditional religions are not primarily for the individual, but for his community of which he is part. Chapters of African religion are written everywhere in the life of the community, and in traditional society there are no irreligious people. To be human is to belong to the whole community, and to do so involves participating in the beliefs, ceremonies, ritual and festivals of that community. A person cannot detach himself from the religion of his group, for to do so is to be severed from his roots, his foundations, his context of security, his kinships and the entire group of those who make him aware of his existence.... To be without religion amounts to a self-excommunication from the entire life of the society, and African peoples do not know how to exist without religion.[7]

This self-understanding was at the core of the world-view of the men, women, and children brought to the United States in chains. It enabled them to bear up under the sudden and shattering catastrophe that had so irrevocably changed their lives and futures. It was this communitarian, holistic, family-based, religious understanding that provided the African slave with a basis for encompassing and accepting, in a somehow richer and more freeing way, the Christianity foisted upon them.[8]

American Branches

It is important and necessary to state again that the Black experience in the U.S. was one of legalized slavery, segregation, second-class citizenship, "Jim-Crow" discrimination,[9] and dehumanization.[10] It was a constant battle against human forces who used every means in their power to subdue and subjugate them into accepting their allegedly Biblically pre-ordained status as "hewers of wood and bearers of water" for the "superior" (white) races. Yet, it is also, and more importantly, an experience of paradox, of the weak managing to triumph in many ways over those opposed to their success at all costs. It is the fulfillment of Paul's prophetic statement that "God chose what is weak in the world to shame the strong; God chose what is low and despised in the world, things that are not, to reduce to nothing things that are" (1 Cor 1:27-28). African Americans in the United States have, historically, been seen as "things," the objects rather than the subjects of their own history.

The theology of African Americans reflects this experience for it is a contextual theology,[11] one which has risen out of the life and death struggles of African Americans to survive, or, in the words of an old gospel song, it is the testimony of "how they got over." Thus, it is the story of their paradoxical encounter with God in extremely negative, life-threatening and soul-denying circumstances and a witness to their profound and deeply-held belief that God was on their side, as God had been on the side of the Hebrew children centuries earlier, marching with them into battle and confusing and confounding their enemies on every side.

Their faith was first revealed, not in theological treatises but in what could be called the "popular religiosity"[12] of the people, their personal expression of faith as revealed in song, prayer and oral narrative. It is first in the spirituals,[13] those soulful songs which expressed both apparent resignation and the determination to survive, in the extemporaneous prayers,[14] and in the witness of their lives and God's abiding and active presence in them[15] that the first halting steps toward an actual Black Liberation Theology can be observed. It is here that the slaves' faith in a Creator God who loved them as God's own children regardless of their color, their faith in God's Son Jesus who fought and continues to fight throughout history the "good fight" on their behalf, the battle for the liberation of all of God's children, and their faith in the Holy Spirit, that pervasive presence of God who inspirits the weak of heart and heals those burdened with "sin-sick" souls, is most poignantly expressed.

The stimuli for their song, their prayer and their witness, which was revealed to them by their faith, were the questions asked in every generation by every oppressed people: "Who is God for us and why have we been afflicted in this way? How can God be for us, as an oppressed and downtrodden people and also be for those who have enslaved and continue to oppress us?" These questions, and others like them, have been raised by

African Americans down through the centuries in their persistent effort to understand, to defend and to pass on their faith while, at the same time, they critique the practical expression of the Christian faith of those who oppressed them, for their faith was one that could not be separated from who they were or how they lived. It was a holistic, lived-out faith which was a part of their very being, as noted earlier. To them, in their understanding of God, it was incomprehensible that the people who enslaved them could believe in the same God and continue to behave as they did. Their disdain and disbelief was revealed when they sang "everybody talkin' 'bout heaven ain't goin' there," disclosing their contempt for the hypocritical witness of faith given them by those who held them in bondage.

The Black Church

A further stimulus for the development of Black Liberation Theology was, and continues to be, the Black Church. Seen historically as those churches which broke away from the established mainline white Protestant churches,[16] they provided a place of refuge but also a resource for gathering strength and returning to the struggle.

> Black Christian preachers realized that God's provident love required that human beings be free to develop their humanity to its fullest potential. If God is free, then human beings, created in the divine image and likeness, were meant to be free. Thus Christian responsibility requires those who have been enslaved to recover their God-given freedom so their *force-vitale*, or inner spirit, could be free.[17]

Today, the persistent Black presence in the predominantly white denominations must also be recognized as an important part of the Black Church, which continues to struggle against marginalization and racism, bringing renewed vigor to the ongoing battle for recognition of the important role Blacks have played in the Christian churches, both in the United States and elsewhere, in the perpetuation of the gospel message of liberation of the poor and oppressed:

> There exists what is called "The Black Church." It crosses denominational boundaries and is without a formal structure. Yet it is a reality cherished by many Black Christians, who feel at ease joining in prayer and in Christian action with one another. This Black Church is a result of our common experience and history—it has made it possible for many Blacks to understand and appreciate each other.[18]

For although it is true that, for some, membership in these churches, especially the Roman Catholic and Episcopalian, could be seen as a way of "getting over" and away from their supposedly less "refined" brothers and sisters, or as a means of assimilating into the mainstream and leaving behind their hated past (and thus, they mistakenly believed, their hated "Blackness"), these Black congregations served, as did their counterparts in the African Methodist Episcopal, African Methodist Episcopal Zion, Christian Methodist Episcopal, Baptist and other churches, as sources of strength, resistance, independence, affirmation, solidarity and encouragement for a people caught in the double bind, as W.E.B. DuBois described it, of being neither fully African nor fully American.[19] However, not all Black Catholics are converts; some trace their faith to the sixteenth century in the United States and to the beginnings of the Church (see endnote 10). The Black Church, from its humble origins in the "hush arbors" of the plantation fields and the self-support organizations of the segregated North, enabled African Americans to persist in maintaining their own expression of faith albeit within the confines of an often restrictive framework laid upon and over it.[20]

It is in the Black Church that the tensions which continue to fluctuate within Black Christianity today have their greatest expression. For it is here that the rhetoric of liberation, "freedom now," had to be tempered, time and time again, by the demands of the status quo. The question of how to agitate for change in a manner and form which would not call down upon them the overwhelming power of the white dominant society, thereby resulting in a worsening rather than an improvement of their lives, was a source of constant debate, both in the pulpits and in the pews. Again, questions of deep significance for their spiritual and physical lives emerged as African Americans asked: "What is God's purpose and meaning for us as people of African descent in a country which seeks to deny our very humanity? How can and should we act as God's agents and live up to the Gospel mandate, in a passive or active way?"[21]

Religion and Radicalism

Few African Americans had the time, the interest or, initially, the education to sit down and develop in a systematic way these embryonic theological dialogues and debates; rather, the questions were raised and the answers were hashed out in fiery discourses and challenging sermons.

Those few who did attempt to articulate and respond to the questions of their day did so from their own perspective of the major issues and concerns confronting their fellow Blacks. Bishop Henry McNeale Turner of the

AME Church contended, as early as 1898, that "God is a Negro" and is, therefore, concerned for the plight of those created in God's own dark image.[22] Bishop Turner called for the repatriation of Black people to their own land of Africa, for he believed they would never be accepted as full human beings in this, their adopted land.[23] He was not alone in this call, for the theme of repatriation, of a return to Africa, is one that arises continuously in the centuries-long history of the peoples of Africa in this land.[24]

Others, like David Walker, appealed to the slaves to overthrow their chains, destroy their masters and mistresses, and become free beings through their own revolutionary actions. Others still, such as Frederick Douglass, worked ceaselessly to influence the hearts and minds of whites in the North and South to protest the continued existence of slavery. To Walker, Douglass, Sojourner Truth, another advocate for abolition, and those like them, the United States, wretched though their lives were in it, had become their new homeland, albeit a strange one, a homeland which had risen to greatness on their shoulders and prospered as a result of their years of unpaid toil and labor.[25]

In later years, the debate would be engaged in by W.E.B. Dubois and Booker T. Washington and their supporters, the former calling forth the "talented tenth" among his Black brothers and sisters to, by their actions, reveal the humanity and ability of all Black peoples and the latter urging his people to learn trades and, in that way, challenge the status quo, thereby achieving, he believed, similar results.[26] DuBois later came to call for a return to Africa and himself settled in Ghana while Washington persisted in his emphasis on a separate but equal status for African Americans in their now native land.[27]

In order to understand, however, the emergence of Black Liberation Theology, it is necessary to further explore the emergence of Black Christianity which serves as the foundation for that theology. Its origins are in the Great Revivals of the eighteenth and nineteenth centuries by which the African slaves, of varying religious traditions, were introduced (or reintroduced) to Christianity and their transformation of it into a liberating and sustaining faith. The discussion, in Chapter Two, will be developed in terms of the life of worship of Black Christians, Protestant and Catholic, for it is here that their faith was formed, developed and passed on.

Notes

1. See Gayraud Wilmore, *Black Religion and Black Radicalism* (Garden City, N.Y.: Doubleday and Co., 1972; second edition, 1983, Orbis Books) which presents in detail this dialectic and its continued presence in Black Christianity.

2. See Forrest G. Wood, *The Arrogance of Faith: Christianity and Race in America from the Colonial Era to the Twentieth Century* (Boston: Northeastern University Press, 1990), and Manning Marable, *Blackwater: Historical Studies in Race, Class Consciousness, and Revolution* (Dayton, Oh: Black Praxis Press, 1981), among others, for a full discussion.

3. The biblical stories of the curse of Cain (Gn 4:10-16) and of the curse of Canaan (Gn 9:20-27) were often cited for the "suitability" of Africans for slavery. Eventually, however, even these aspects of humanity were denied as slaves became classified as "three-fifths of a person" in the Constitution, as chattel in the same sense as livestock and crops, and, as stated by the U.S. Supreme Court in the Dred Scott decision (19 Howard 393, 1857), African Americans were "so far inferior that they had no rights which a white man was bound to respect." See, for example Wood, chs. 1–3.

4. The major slave rebellions that are known were those of Gabriel Prosser, Denmark Vesey, and Nat Turner, all of whom were led by their reading of the Bible to believe their captivity was unjust and against the will of God. Hundreds of other rebellions took place as well resulting, finally, in the passage of Black Codes which denied literacy, the freedom to gather and hold their own church services and other rights to the slaves. There are a number of excellent histories of African Americans, including those by Lerone Bennett, *Before The Mayflower* (New York: Penguin Books, 1993, 6th rev. ed.); John Hope Franklin, *From Slavery to Freedom: A History of Negro Americans* (New York: Alfred J. Knopf, 1980, 5th ed.); Vincent Harding, *There Is a River: The Black Struggle for Freedom in America* (New York and London: Harcourt Brace Jovanovich, 1981) and Mary Berry and John W. Blassingame, *Long Memory: The Black Experience in America* (New York and Oxford: Oxford University Press, 1982), among others.

5. While some assert that Blacks in the U.S. have become, in actuality, a nation within a nation—see, for example, Andrew Hacker, *Two Nations, Black and White, Separate and Unequal* (N.Y.: Charles Scribner's Sons, 1992)—others such as Henry Louis Gates, Jr., while agreeing that Blacks are a nation in and of themselves, note that it is a nation divided, especially along class lines; see his "Two Nations...Both Black" in Robert Gooding-Williams, ed., *Reading Rodney King, Reading Urban Uprising* (N.Y.: Routledge, 1993), pp. 249-254. Although Black America has never been the uniform monolith that many, especially those outside of the Black community, have assumed, it must be acknowledged that the former solidarity which once enabled that community to maintain itself against numerous onslaughts has been weakened, paradoxically, since the end of the Civil Rights Movement; see, for example, Cornel West's discussion of "the nihilistic threat" to the existence of Black America in *Race Matters* (N.Y.: Vintage Books, 1994), ch. 1, pp. 17-31.

6. Africans were farmers, hunters and grazers, warriors, builders of huts and stone buildings, lived in villages and cities and developed nations and empires such as Egypt, Mali, Songhay, Ghana, and Timbuktu which rivaled those of Rome and Greece with which they traded and engaged in commerce, both commercial and intellectual. See Cheikh Ante Diop, *The African Origins of Civilization: Myth or Reality* (Chicago: Lawrence Hill Books, 1974, originally published Paris: Presence Africaine, 1967), and Basil Davidson, author of many works on Africa including *African Civilization Revisited* (N.Y.: African World Press, 1991) and *The Lost Cities of Africa* (Boston: Little, Brown and Co., 1987, rev. ed.).

7. John S. Mbiti, *African Religions and Philosophy* (Garden City, N.Y.: Doubleday Anchor Books, 1970), p. 3.

8. See Jamie Phelps, O.P., "Black Spirituality," in Robin Maas and Gabriel O'Donnell, O.P., *Spiritual Traditions for the Contemporary Church* (Nashville: Abingdon Press, 1990).

9. C. Vann Woodward in *The Strange Career of Jim Crow* (N.Y.: Oxford University Press, 1955; 3rd rev. ed., 1974) notes: "The origin of the term 'Jim Crow' applied to Negroes is lost in obscurity. Thomas D. Rice wrote a song and dance called 'Jim Crow' in 1832, and the term had become an adjective by 1838. The first example of 'Jim Crow law' listed by the *Dictionary of American English* is dated 1904. But the expression was used by writers in the 1890's...." Jim Crow laws were the segregation statutes which, Woodward notes, "constituted the most elaborate and formal expression of sovereign white opinion upon the subject" (p. 7, Intro.) of Black inferiority legally and racially.

10. It should be noted, however, that the first Africans in what is now the United States arrived in the Southwest in 1565 with the Spanish conquistadors and were among the founders of St. Augustine, Fl., Los Angeles, Ca. and other cities, Spanish or French in origin. Many were free, not enslaved. The 1619 date usually cited is for the English-speaking, Protestant colonies.

See Cyprian Davis, O.S.B., *The History of Black Catholics in the United States* (N.Y.: Crossroad, 1990), ch. 1.

11. Stephen Bevans in his *Models of a Contextual Theology* (Maryknoll, N.Y.: Orbis, 1992) sees contextual theology as "a way of doing theology in which one takes into account: the spirit and message of the Gospel; the tradition of the Christian people; the culture in which one is theologizing; and social change in that culture, whether brought about by western technological process or the grass-roots struggle for equality, justice and liberation." Doing contextual theology is not an option nor is it something that should only interest people from the Third World or missionaries who work there. The contextualization of theology—the attempt to understand Christian faith in terms of a particular context—is really a theological imperative. As we understand theology today, contextualization is part of the very nature of theology itself.

12. This religiosity was initially "invisible" but has today been revealed in the slave and ex-slave narratives and other sources: see especially the work by Dwight Hopkins in this area; with George Cummings, eds. *Cut Loose Your Stammering Tongues: Black Theology and the Slave Narratives* (Maryknoll, N.Y.: Orbis, 1992) and *Shoes That Fit Our Feet: Sources for a Constructive Black Theology* (Maryknoll, N.Y.: Orbis, 1993), as well as Albert Raboteau, *Slave Religion: The "Invisible" Institution in the Antebellum South* (N.Y.: Oxford University Press, 1978) and Lawrence Levine, *Black Culture and Black Consciousness* (N.Y.: Oxford University Press, 1977) particularly chs. 1 and 2.

13. James Cone in his, at that time, innovative work, *The Spirituals and the Blues* (New York: The Seabury Press, 1972), explores in great depth the theological significance of Black music, both secular and religious. Other sources include Eileen Southern, *The Music of Black America* (N.Y.: Norton, 2nd ed., 1983); John Lowell, *Black Song: The Forge and the Flame* (N.Y.: Paragon House, 1986); Dwight Hopkins and George

Cummings, eds., *Cut Loose*, and Hopkins, *Shoes*; Jon Spence, *Black Hymnody* (Knoxville, TN:, University of Tennessee Press, 1992) and *Protest and Praise: Sacred Music of Black Religion* (Minneapolis: Fortress Press, 1990); and Arthur Jones, *Wade in the Water: The Wisdom of the Spirituals* (Maryknoll, N.Y.: Orbis, 1993). Although initially thought by many scholars to be passive and ethereal, looking toward a future reward in heaven (see for example the classic by Benjamin Mays, *The Negro's God as Reflected in His Literature* (Greenwood Pr., 1970, originally published 1938), more recent scholarship has revealed the slaves' emphasis on liberation in the present and the double-meanings hidden in the spirituals which not only gave the slaves the strength to persevere but also encouraged them in their flight from and rebellion against slavery.

14. See James Melvin Washington, *Conversations with God: Two Centuries of Prayers by African Americans* (New York: HarperCollins, 1994); Harold Carter, *The Prayer Tradition of Black People* (Baltimore: Gateway Press, 1982); Henry Mitchell and Nicholas Lewter, *Soul Theology: The Heart of American Black Culture* (Nashville: Abingdon, 1991); *Black Belief* (N.Y.: Harper and Row, 1975), and *Black Preaching* (N.Y.: Harper and Row, 1970); and Hopkins, *Shoes*, among others who reveal how the prayers and sermons of slaves are a rich source for understanding their encounter with God and how that encounter was made manifest in their midst.

15. See Hopkins and Cummings, ed., *Cut Loose*, and Clifton Johnson, ed. *God Struck Me Dead: Voices of the Ex-Slaves* (Cleveland: Pilgrim Press, 1993; 1st pub. 1969).

16. The first known Black church was Baptist, founded in Silver Bluff, South Carolina in the mid to late 1770s and it remained active for some time before and after the Revolutionary War. Other independent Black churches emerged in the South but few were free to remain so until after the Civil War when the then "Colored," now Christian Methodist Episcopal Church formed by separating from the Southern

Methodist Church. See the interesting article by Walter Brooks, "The Priority of the Silver Bluff Church and Its Promoters," in *The Journal of Negro History* 7 (1922) 172-196. In the North, however, two churches arose, the African Methodist Episcopal, founded in Philadelphia, PA by Richard Allen and other freemen (1794), and the African Methodist Episcopal Zion founded by James Varick and others in New York City (1821). Both arose due to the refusal of white congregations to treat their Black members as equals in the church. Baptist churches also developed in the North as well. The Roman Catholic Church, because of its institutional structure, did not develop separate Black churches nor did other predominantly white churches, although Black parishes, headed by white priests or ministers, did emerge especially after the Civil War.

17. Jamie Phelps, O.P., "Black Spirituality," in *Spiritual Traditions*, p. 340.

18. Black Bishops of the United States, *What We Have Seen and Heard: A Pastoral Letter on Evangelization* (Cincinnati, Ohio: St. Anthony Messenger Press, 1984), p. 15.

19. "It is a peculiar sensation, this double consciousness, this sense of always looking at one's self through the eyes of others, of measuring one's self through the eyes of others, of one's soul by the tape of a world that looks on in amused contempt and pity. One ever feels his twoness—an American, a Negro; two souls, two thoughts, two unreconciled strivings; two warring ideals in one dark body, whose dogged strength alone keeps it from being torn asunder." "Of Our Spiritual Strivings," in *The Souls of Black Folk* (New York: NAL, Signet Classic, 1969), p. 45. A recent work which both affirms and challenges this perspective is Gerald Early, ed., *Lure and Loathing: Essays on Race, Identity, and the Ambivalence of Assimilation* (New York: Penguin Books, 1993).

20. See Diana L. Hayes, "Black Catholic Revivalism: The Emergence of A New Form of Worship," in *The Journal of the*

Interdenominational Theological Center, Vol. 14 (Fall 1986/ Spring 1987),#1/2, pp. 87-107 as well as Chapter Two of this work.

21. See Gayraud Wilmore for a more in-depth discussion of these two poles of Black Christianity, in his *Black Religion and Black Radicalism*, especially Chapter 9.

22. Edwin S. Redkey, *Respect Black: The Writings and Teachings of Henry McNeale Turner* (New York: Seabury, 1971), p. 177.

23. See Lerone Bennett, *Before the Mayflower*, p. 285.

24. Supporters varied from Presidents Jefferson and Lincoln to prominent politicians, abolitionists and, as with Turner, Blacks themselves, such as Alexander Crummell, John Russwurm, Henry Highland Garnet, and Martin R. Delany. All of these men were active in the Colored Convention movement which began in Philadelphia in 1830 but eventually migrated to Africa. See Delany, *The Condition, Elevation, and Destiny of the Colored People of the United States, Politically Considered* (Salem, N.H.: Ayer Press, reprint of 1852 edition), and Garnet, "An Address to the Slaves of the United States of America" (1843) as well as pro and con statements re migration by John Russwurm and Richard Allen in Deirdre Mullane, ed. *Crossing the Danger Water: Three Hundred Years of African American Writing* (N.Y.: Anchor Doubleday, 1993), pp. 115-121, 67-73. All of this was instrumental in the founding of the African nation of Liberia which, in actuality, until the recent bloody civil wars, in many ways was simply a colony of the U.S., dependent upon it economically and politically. As recently as the present decade, the call to return to the homeland, either physically or in spirit through dress, hair styles, language, and festivals, has been set forth by Minister Louis Farrakhan of the Nation of Islam (a physical return) and others.

25. See *Walker's Appeal in Four Articles* as excerpted in Mullane, *Danger Water*, pp. 76-85; Frederick Douglass, *Autobi-*

ographies (N.Y.: The Library of America, 1994 and "What to the Negro Is the Fourth of July?" (1852) in Mullane, pp. 157-160; and Sojourner Truth, "Address to the Ohio Women's Rights Convention" (1851) and "Address to the First Annual Meeting of the American Equal Rights Association (1867) in Mullane, pp. 184-188.

26. See W.E.B. DuBois, "The Talented Tenth" (1903) in Mullane, pp. 382-392 and "Of Mr. Booker T. Washington and Others" in *The Souls of Black Folk* (N.Y.: Literary Classics of the United States, 1986) and Booker T. Washington, "The Atlanta Exposition Address" (1895), in Mullane, pp. 364-367 and *Up From Slavery* (N.Y.: Penguin, 1986, orig. 1901).

27. The "Back to Africa" movement and the "call to revolution" (Black Nationalism) can be seen as further examples of the dipolarity which persists in the Black historical experience to the present day. On the one hand, a return to Africa can be seen as a passive acquiescence in the belief that Blacks do not and never will belong in the U.S. and therefore should return from whence they came. It fails, however, to acknowledge that the Black presence in the United States was not and never had been in its origins a voluntary presence. On the other hand, the persistent calls for resistance and revolt and the adamant refusal to return to a country which, by this time, most African Americans had no knowledge of or affinity with can be seen both in the earlier slave rebellions and in the emergence of the Black Power and Black Nationalist movements of the 1960s. Washington's emphasis on being as "separate as the fingers on one hand" but as united economically as that hand "balled into a fist" fits into the pacifist camp, yet, at the same time, his actions in founding Tuskeegee Institute in Tuskeegee, Alabama laid the foundation for the emergence of Blacks capable of leadership in various fields of endeavor.

2

Revivals and
Parish Missions[1]

The religious phenomenon known as a "revival of religion" or "revivalism" is rooted in the European awakenings which led to religious and political upheavals, and resulted in the flight or forced emigration of many who were believed to observe the "wrong" religious practices (for example, the Pilgrims).

Those who fled eventually to the New World brought with them a religion rigidly strict in its beliefs and observances. The Puritans (descendants of a strict Calvinism) prayed to an omnipotent God who predestined those elected to be saved and damned all others, regardless of the quality of their lives. This belief, or ethic, was to dominate the political and social life of the United States long after the Puritans themselves ceased to exist and is still a strong undercurrent in American Christianity. This has led to a society "where Darwinism has been attached to Calvinism in such a way that human life is not only seen as survival of the fittest, but that the fittest are seen as deserving, even being destined, to survive."[2]

This sovereign, austere form of faith and worship did not fit this country, with its vast wealth of seemingly vacant land and other resources which promised prosperity to all who were strong and hardworking. The freedom to work and think for oneself in secular affairs led inevitably to thinking for oneself on religious matters as well and a resulting decline in Puritanism's controlling influence. The seeds for the First Great Awakening were planted.[3]

Protestant Revivalism

There have been at least two Great Awakenings or "revivals of religion" in American history. (Both names will be used interchangeably hereafter.)

The first, occurring between 1730-1760, caused the first signs of strain in the seamless fabric of the Puritan Church. The second, between 1800 and 1830, witnessed the final schism in the Puritan Church and the birth or strengthening of the Methodist, Baptist, and other "evangelical" denominations. This period also saw the beginnings of the Black Church, as already noted. It is these two Awakenings which were critical to the formation of a Black Christianity that partook of both the Christian faith as imposed, usually in a restricted or distorted form, on the African slaves and the deep faith and religiosity already present within them from their African past.

Why do "revivals of religion" occur? Not simply because of dissatisfaction with any particular Church's teachings. Nor are they merely religious upheavals which arise only to fade away leaving all untouched. Rather, they encompass political and social problems as well. Not limited to any particular culture, race, religion, or class, religious revivals spread throughout a nation, overturning everything in their tracks:

> They are essentially folk movements, the means by which a people or nation reshapes its identity, trans-

forms its patterns of thought and action, and sustains a healthy relationship with environmental and social change.[4]

Revivals are only one manifestation of many which occur in the phenomena of a Great Awakening:

> Great Awakenings (and the Revivals that are part of them) are the result, not of depressions, wars, or epidemics, but of ontical disjunctions in our self understanding. They are not brief outbursts of mass emotionalism by one group or another but profound cultural transformations affecting all Americans and extending over a generation or more. Awakenings begin in periods of cultural distortion and grave personal stress, when we lose faith in the legitimacy of our norms, the viability of our institutions and the authority of our leaders in Church and state. They eventuate in basic restructuring of our institutions and redefinitions of our social goals.[5]

The first Great Awakening was a reaction against the established order which had evolved from the English Reformation. It was a "revitalizing" movement in English society which offered a new code of beliefs and values more in harmony with the needs and experiences of the rising middle class over against the aristocracy. The "Protestant (work) ethic,"[6] in revolt against the medieval practices still employed by the Anglican church with its condemnation of usury (interest on loans) and individual initiative as opposed to the trade and craft guilds, established a new set of virtues which enabled the flourishing of capitalistic practices.

It was a political and religious movement based on Sacred Scripture as the sole authority for all human and social action. Seeking to be even more restrictive than their Calvinistic forebears, the Puritans stressed predestination, hard work and sober observance of the law for the benefit of the entire community.

This was the religious mindset brought to America by its first colonists, one which favored self-sacrifice for the common good and the subjection of individual freedoms to the will of the community, a good and community reserved, however, for the Elect. Free will did not exist and only a few "elect" were assured of the joys of heaven. Individual initiative and success on the latter's part was considered evidence of their election.

The first strains in this theology, and the non-elect's adherence to it, began with the opening of the frontier territories. As families moved into these new lands, they found that with diligence and patience they could make better lives for themselves. The Church's influence and power, which was supported by universal taxation, was weakened by distance. Class barriers began to bend and then break as the new landowners began to recognize their own equality and status. Estrangement between the common people and their Church and state leaders grew as the non-elect began to question a world-view which condemned the majority to hell and maintained the reins of power and authority in the hands of a few.

As noted earlier, theology emerges in response to the questions people ask about God and their relationship to God. A new spirit of intimacy with God emerged which believers sought to share with others of like mind. Rather than waiting on the Lord passively, they believed that God would respond to their prayers and actions. This sense of participation in one's own salvation led to the creation of "new churches and sects, new forms of Christian fellowship."[7]

By 1740, revivals had spread across the colonies. Itinerant preachers, especially those from England, came with a new style of rhetorical preaching which appealed directly to the audience's emotions. They called each person individually back to God, thereby redefining God's relationship in a very personal way to each sinner. As a part of this awakening of the Spirit, colonists began to feel more in touch not only with God but with themselves and with the world around them, leading to a revolution in religious, social, and political practices. Individuals took ownership of their own lives and spirituality; the result was a democratization of religion and the shattering of class lines. The authority of the ordained over the political, social and religious lives of the people was broken. ❧

The Methodist sect, originally a part of Anglicanism, was strengthened by this "revival of religion." With their stress on universal salvation and their innovative method of evangelization by means of itinerant evangelists and lay preachers, Methodism was the answer for those dissatisfied with the restrictions of the colonial governments. The world-view of the Calvinists, with its stress on human depravity and one's inability to improve one's lot, came increasingly in conflict with the world-view of Enlightenment rationalism, which saw mankind as innately good and able to better its situation through individual actions. This latter view was to emerge victorious from the struggle.

The American revolution temporarily slowed this religious and social ferment but it re-emerged with the Second Great Awakening (1800-1830). Once again, the fear arose that the country was falling away from religion. With the passage of the Bill of Rights, separation of Church and state became law. Many of the founding fathers of the new nation were more inclined to deistic and rationalistic views than the image of the U.S. as the new Promised Land. The growing expansion of an apparently "irreligious" western frontier increased the fears that the nation would soon become totally atheistic or secular.

Protestant ministers hoped for a second "revival of religion." This time, however, the clergy would be promoters, rather than bystanders. Although still hampered by their pantheistic belief that a revival was a "miracle" of God and could not be brought about by human effort, yet they believed that prayer and patience would eventually succeed.

In the West, however, the children of the First Awakening had abandoned such a restrictive outlook. Between 1798 and 1810, there took place, especially in Kentucky, a passionate outburst of the Spirit known as the Western or Kentucky revival. Although revivals were still considered to be miracles and individual conversion, "a work of God outside the sequence of natural events,"[8] many came to acknowledge that human instigation could be the yeast which began the fermentation.

The Western revival brought about a further revolution in religious thought. Conversion was considered to be an individual act available to all, "a personal change of heart which came about suddenly and publicly and under excruciating emotional pressure."[9] Individual conversion became the culmination of the Christian experience for each person. "Only those who were born again and went through a conversion experience were saved; all others, regardless of their virtue or piety, were sinners."[10] On the surface, this was a new version of the elect/non-elect teachings of the Puritans, but with a major difference: conversion was available to all, regardless of race, class, or gender.

Conversion was the important thing. It was an emotional overhauling of the sinner, usually manifested by dancing in the aisles, experiencing the "jerks" and "shudders," or falling away in a prolonged faint lasting hours or even days. Many felt the need to exhort their fellow sinners to confess their sins and to follow the straight and narrow path of God.

The preacher's role became more active. Eighteenth century preaching had been intellectual and didactic, but by the early nineteenth century, it had become a fiery exhortation meant "to convulse the conscience" of the repentant convert. The preacher "sharpened the message of man's guilt to a point, by repetition, and drove it into the sinner's heart.... The sinner had to feel in his very bones the smoldering of guilt, abasement, hope, and assurance."[11]

The Methodists gained the most converts. In their opposition to Calvinistic predestination and in their enthusiastic "camp-meetings," the peoples of the violent frontier felt welcomed, at home, and free to express themselves.

The movement was also slowly taking over the East but in a more subdued manner. Here, conversion was still considered an exercise of the mind rather than of the heart. Attempts were made to redefine Calvinist theology to provide more room for personal activity. The portrayal of an arbitrary and sovereign God slowly gave way to one of a God who governed through moral principles to which all people, with his help, might be able to conform. A peripheral but critical result of these theological changes was the growing recognition of the Christian's responsibility to participate in social and community activities.

At this critical juncture, Charles Grandison Finney came upon the scene (1820-1830), bringing the "lusty breath of the Western revival into the East."[12] Finney changed the face of the newly emerging evangelicalism with his views on social reform and conversion. Having no interest in waiting upon the Lord to get things started, he saw "a revival of religion...not (as) a miracle"[13] nor dependent upon any miracle. It was, rather, the result of the "right use of the appropriate means,"[14] but always with the blessing of God. It was Finney's contention that

> almost all the religion in the world has been produced by revivals. God has found it necessary to take advantage of the excitability there is in mankind, to produce powerful excitements among them, before he can lead them to obey.[15]

Finney and his successors claimed immediate conversion in front of the altar. People were accepted or converted completely and immediately without having to wait "in hope" for confirmation on the final day of judgment. Revivals became events not "rained down" by the grace of God, but planned and run by professional evangelists who preached and planned them with a flair for detail down to the number and color of altar flowers. Accompanying these changes came an increased use of music, especially participatory congregational hymns, which became the backbone of all revivals.

It was at this point that the churches and evangelists began to look beyond the internal problems of their churches to the sinful state of the world around them. Evangelization became the purpose of the Protestant Church as it sought to save mankind by "giving universal and saving empire to the Kingdom of Christ."[16] As the revival fervor began to fade, its energy was transferred to the growing antislavery, temperance, and other social movements.

By the 1890s, the foundations of Evangelical Protestantism were well in place. It was a religion, especially as exemplified by the Methodist and Baptist denominations, which upheld the verbal inspiration, inerrancy, and sole authority of the Scriptures. It also emphasized the supreme importance of proclaiming the Word of God in preaching while reducing liturgical worship to the barest minimum.

Evangelical Protestantism was not merely a back-woods illiterate religion which appealed solely to the emotions, however. The circuit-riders were well-versed in their creed which was founded on the belief that all could be saved and reconciled to God through Christ. However, it was not an intellectual religion, either. It spoke to the heart of the individual sinner in terms which they could understand. Its theology was based on a realism which provided a clear distinction between right and wrong, good and evil. It stressed the value of the individual and the significance of the emotions in mankind and modified the doctrine of original sin to allow for progressive reform which gave rise to the political benevolence movement (social reform). Above all, evangelicals stressed the immanence of God as Spirit.

Black Protestant Revivalism

The new sense of social reform which developed among Protestants soon began to focus on the conditions of the Negro slaves.

> The revivalism of the Great Awakening, spread over time and space by evangelical preachers, created the conditions for large-scale conversion of the slaves. By revitalizing the religious piety of the South, the Awakening(s) stirred an interest in conversion which was turned toward the slaves. By heavily emphasizing the inward conversion experience, the Awakening tended to de-emphasize the outward status of men and to cause Black and white alike to feel personally that Christ had died for them as individuals. Evangelical religion had a universal-

istic dimension which encouraged preaching to all men, embracing rich and poor, free and slave. The emotionalism and plain doctrine of revivalist preaching appealed to the masses, including the slaves.[17]

After the American revolution, Anglicanism was uprooted in the South and replaced by Evangelicalism. With its stress on the "primacy of religious experience, the conviction of sin, the need for repentance and the importance of close fellowship and discipline,"[18] it soon swept the area. The problem that evolved was "how to preach a Gospel premised on individual autonomy within the framework of slavery."[19]

No serious attempts had been made to convert the slaves until the problem of the effect of Baptism was settled to the satisfaction of slaveholders. Only when the established churches decreed that conversion resulted in a spiritual, rather than physical, freedom did evangelization really begin.[20] Slavery was instituted in the "new world" for economic reasons, although the reason usually given was the "conversion of the pagan Africans."

Attempts were made to grant at least a "spiritual personhood" to the slaves despite their alleged "inferiority."[20a] However, many planters resisted the evangelization of their human "property" because of their fears of the effect conversion would have on them, especially in bolstering rather than dampening their pride and rebelliousness.[21] Still, for others, especially those in ministry to the slaves, Black evangelization was seen as a "balm for Southern conscience" and a means of keeping the slaves in line.[22] This justification was explicitly expressed by Charles C. Pinckney in an address to southern planters in 1829:

Were true religion propagated among this numerous and important class, a sense of duty would counteract their reluctance to labour, and, diminishing the cases of feigned sickness so harassing to the Planter, would augment their numerical force and consequent production. The social relations of life being better observed, a greater proportion of domestic happiness would prevail and render them more contented with their situation, and more anxious to promote their owner's welfare. The absence, or diminution of theft, falsehood, and many other vices, would render the home of the Agriculturalist far more agreeable than it can be, where guilt, which escapes human detection, knows not, and fears not, another tribunal.[23]

The Christianity which developed as an outcome of such thinking was one that confused the temporal sphere with the spiritual, which sought to make good saints out of good servants and expressed itself in a hope for a better future in which the "troubles of this world" would "soon be over." The present-day situation and injustices were glossed over. Certain scriptural texts were emphasized, such as Paul's Epistle to Philemon, and similar readings which stressed the duties of servant to master, the God-given mandate of obedience to one's superiors, and the necessity that one rest in the state in which one found oneself without agitating for a change in one's situation (cf. 1 Cor 7:20-24; Eph 6:5-7 Tit 2:9), while others, especially any referring to liberation, were ignored or glossed over.

Those slaves who were converted did not accept their indoctrination unquestioningly, especially when they were initially allowed to read for themselves and were given access to the Bible. They were often critical of the hypocrisy underlying Christianity as it was taught to them. They did not trust, initially, a religion which held them to virtues they saw being blatantly ignored by their masters. As they read other sections of the Bible, a change in their understanding and acceptance took place.

They were able somehow to differentiate between the piety of those around them and what they saw as the true virtues of the Christian religion. From these insights, a liberating piety emerged, one which allowed them to survive, without, however, adding to their oppression.

Timothy Smith suggests that

> the Christian beliefs they adopted enabled the African exiles to endure slavery precisely because these beliefs supported their moral revulsion toward it and promised eventual deliverance from it without demanding that they risk their lives in immediate resistance.[24]

However, resist they did, as the increasing number of revolts led by Christian slaves attests.

Initially, Southern religious life was integrated with both Blacks and whites gathering for the same camp-meetings and experiencing the "convulsions" of the Spirit together. Black preachers were often encouraged and ordained by both Baptists and Methodists, and Black exhorters, deacons or watchmen were set up on each plantation to "conduct evening prayers...assist church members by warnings, reproofs, and exhortations, heal breaches, report cases of delinquency, see that children be taught their prayers, and that everybody attended worship."[25] The Black ministers not only preached to Black or mixed congregations, but were often allowed, because of their scriptural knowledge and fervent preaching style, to "exhort" totally white congregations.

However, even during this period many slaves still preferred to conduct their own "hush-arbor" gatherings. These usually took place late at night and were events characterized by singing, handclapping, oral prayer, and fervent preaching, all culminating in communal ecstasy. In these sessions, Blacks felt they could more freely be themselves. It is from these clandestine gatherings that the first meshings of African traditional religions and Protestant Christianity occurred.

As noted earlier, when the African peoples, uprooted from their ancestral homes in Africa, were brought to the United States in chains, they did not lose all that they had known and loved of their ancient culture. They were a religious people long before they had any contact with "civilization."

> The African beliefs in one Supreme Being, in a realistic distinction between good and evil, in lesser spiritual powers, and in creation paralleled much in the Hebrew background of Christianity.[26]

This religious background helped ameliorate the cultural shock of their first exposure to the tenets of white evangelicalism. It is important to stress that these African roots were not erased or eliminated by that exposure. Rather, after a period of time, they "incorporated into their Christianity certain beliefs and practices which paralleled those of the traditional tribal cults."[27]

With the increasing slave rebellions in the late eighteenth and early nineteenth centuries, led by men like Nat Turner, a slave who was allowed to travel and preach, and others, such as Gabriel Prosser and Denmark Vesey, who rebelled against their status and felt "called" by God to free their people as well as the growing Northern agitation against slavery, much of the slaves' freedom to worship was abruptly ended.[28] In a matter of weeks, harsh and oppressive laws were passed in the Southern states which forbade the teaching of reading and writing to them and which stripped Black ministers of their right to preach and gather a Church.

These restrictions severely crippled religious freedom and activity for Blacks in the South until after the Civil War. Once-thriving Churches were closed, often violently. Religion in the South became, with rare exceptions, white-dominated and white-oriented. The observance of Black religious services took place out of sight of the masters, at night, in the fields or not at all.[29]

What type of religious beliefs were the outgrowth of this paradoxical admixture of freedom and oppression? They were beliefs expressed in terms of the paradox and mystery of God's dealings with mankind. There was an intertwining of emotion with perception which led to a unique theology of hope. Theirs was not a religion of complacency or compensation. Nor was it merely a religion which looked only to "pie in the sky when I die." Rather, it was a faith rooted in an encounter with injustice from which sprang a theology of God's mysterious exercise of sovereignty over human history expressed in judgment and forgiveness, but, most of all, in love. As James Cone noted, speaking of his upbringing in Bearden, Arkansas in the first half of this century:

> For some...who do not know existentially the Black religious experience, the survival and identity emphasis of Black religion will surely validate their claim that it is an opiate. There are of course many Black churches that are vulnerable to the Marxist critique. But I would claim that to apply the label of opiate to Black religion in Bearden during my early years is to be doctrinaire and superficial, neglecting to probe the depths of the Black experience that gave birth to the church.
>
> Furthermore, labeling religion a mere pain-killer ignores the Black church as the source, not only of identity and survival, but of the sociopolitical struggle for liberation.[30]

The slaves took the stories of the Fall of Adam and Eve, of Moses, of Mary, and of the Cross and interpreted them in the light of their own encounters with despair and hope:

> Moses became the deliverer of an enslaved people as well as the bearer of the Ten Commandments. Jonah's trembling denunciation of the sin of the Ninevites affirmed their suspicion that the rich and powerful were not necessarily God's chosen. Biblical accounts of the conduct of believing Jews during the Babylonian exile— of Daniel, of the three who would not bow down, and of Esther the Queen—seemed to Christian Blacks, as to generations of Jews, to be allegories of promise to the oppressed. The baby Jesus, needing tenderness and care, revealed a God whose love made him somehow vulnerable and dependent, and weakness of human faith joined him forever with the meek who would inherit the earth.[31]

The African slaves transformed the Protestant faith while, at the same time, transforming themselves into a new people: African Americans. The emphasis was still on the individual and his or her own singular conversion. However, the Old Testament doctrine of a chosen people was adapted "in such a way as to affirm a common humanity rather than their people's separateness."[32] For them, Christianity was a "reaching out" to affirm themselves and others, as they traveled hand-in-hand with the Lord Jesus on his pain-strewn path to glory. From these roots came an outpouring of self-respect and spiritual authority which sustained many Black Christians in their struggle against the temptation to accept the white man's estimate of their worth.

Christianity, as they adapted it, enabled them to withstand the constant blows struck against them, both before and after emancipation. As an unknown freed woman put it: "My soul was set free long before the fetters fell from my body. God gave me his freedom, but the little children of this earth would not give me theirs."[33]

As a result of their unwilling arrival upon American soil, the slaves had to look beyond their masters to those who shared their burden and oppression. Fellow slaves who would never have been called brother or sister in Africa were bound together in the common goal of saving their lives and preserving their humanity. From this unity came a religious conversion which stressed human solidarity and community rather than individual freedom. This solidarity laid the foundation for the triumphs of the Black Church in the twentieth century.

The renewed Christianity which emerged from this transformation of Protestant piety into a uniquely Black piety was also unique in other ways. It was characterized, especially in the South after the Civil War, by the "Old-Time Revival": an outdoor experience of communality and spiritualization similar in its fervor to the earlier camp meetings from which it grew. The Black conversion experience meant "getting religion," having a special kind of experience during which one was touched by the hand of God and permanently changed.

The "Old-Time Revival" was characterized by individual denunciation of sin in a public confession, an experience which could sometimes take several days. The minister and the "saints" of the Church needed that time to decide whether the person had truly experienced God's healing grace. Those seeking that grace sat on the Mourner's Bench at the front of the Church and were exhorted, preached at, sung to, and prayed over with unceasing fervor until the Spirit hit them.

The most important aspects of these events were the emphasis on singing, the preaching which dragged the sinner from the fiery furnaces of hell to the pearly gates of glory, and the community itself. Everyone was involved in some way, either as preacher, witnesser, usher, choir member, food preparer, repentant sinner, or pray-er. It was a family affair which provided nurturing for the extended family and strength for Black people through hard times.

In short, it was a doxology of song, prayer and preaching. It was a soul-stimulating, soul-satisfying experience which manifested the spirit of the transcendent God present in their midst. It laid the "foundation for the development of a God-fearing and humane Black religious community."[34]

The Roman Catholic world was not immune to the "revivals of religion" taking place throughout the land. Catholics, too, experienced a period of revivalism similar to that of the Protestants, resulting in what can be called a "sacramental evangelicalism" which found a home, especially, among Black Catholics.[35]

Roman Catholic Revivalism

Contrary to the view too often given by many Euro-American religious historians, the Roman Catholic Church and its people also experienced a revival movement during the second half of the nineteenth century. Most revival historians speak only of Protestant Awakenings, with minimal reference to the Roman Catholic Church. However, the Catholic parish mission can also be considered as a form of revival with many of the same characteristics of a Protestant evangelical revival. Similarities include stress on individual conversion, a theology of individualism rooted in repentance, and fervently emotional preaching. There were differences as well, particularly the Catholic emphasis on inclusion of the Sacrament of Penance (Confession, now known as the Sacrament of Reconciliation) in the personal experience of conversion and in the pre-eminence of the celebration of the Eucharist. In its own way, Catholic revivalism gave birth to a form of evangelicalism, a "sacramental evangelicalism," which "shaped the piety of the people and strengthened the universal church."[36]

The Catholic revival was conceived in the parish mission, a form of evangelism dating back to the sixteenth and seventeenth centuries in Europe. As the Great Awakenings were the result of a growing disjunction between church, state, and people, the Catholic missions were a result of an increasing "religious malaise" among both clergy and congregations as well as the tensions and upheavals in thought and practice which resulted from the Protestant Reformation. In both cases, the need for a spiritual overhaul was evident.

The parish mission was also the result of a new preaching style developed by religious orders founded during the Catholic Counter-Reformation. The Jesuits were the initiators who brought structure and form to the mission concept, which preached the burning fires of hell and the need for individual repentance and conversion.

Missions appeared on the American continent with representatives of the different orders of priests, especially the Jesuits, Redemptorists, and Passionists, who were sent to minister to the needs of the fledgling American Church. The first probably took place in Maryland near the end of the eighteenth century.[37]

Catholicism, as with Protestantism, was in a very derelict condition in the early 1800s:

> Too few parishes, not enough priests and a population either scattered across the frontier or densely con-centrated in the city were not conditions favorable to

consolidation of a missionary church. Coupled with this was the obvious pattern of religious neglect among Catholic Americans.[38]

Far away from their former parish church, with the possibility of seeing a priest, if fortunate, perhaps once a year, there was a gradual but definite falling away from religious observance of the tenets of faith by Catholic immigrants.

Most Catholics, however, looked down upon the Protestant form of revivalism, especially the Methodist camp meetings, as "heathenish" assemblies. The clergy, in particular, were opposed to religious enthusiasm as an end in itself. It was felt that, "in Protestant revivals, excitement is carried to excess, and made the end aimed at. In Catholic retreats and missions, it is wisely managed and made simply a means."[39] In actuality, they were not that different in conception, purpose or practice.

As with the camp meetings, often the parish mission was held wherever a large group of people could be congregated. On the frontier, this meant huge tents, open fields, or barns. Both aimed for conversion, the reclaiming of sinners for Jesus Christ, and were "specially calculated to excite the piety of the faithful."[40] Stress was on the spoken word, often accompanied by a "variety of theatrical techniques." The mission was preached with "powerful emotion" and often the audiences responded with spontaneous outbursts of weeping, shuddering and moaning. Catholic revival preachers were also itinerant circuit riders. Initially, emphasis was on the already baptized but fallen-away Catholics. The revival was an occasion for conversion of the indifferent, the new immigrants who had recently come from Europe and who were failing rapidly in their faith.

The Paulists, the first indigenous religious order in

the United States, were established specifically to run parish missions. They acknowledged:

A mission...is something which gathers into one powerful showing all the warnings of Divine Justice fully explaining the enormous folly and ingratitude of sin; it leads the sinner back to his very childhood and traces his downward track through youth and manhood towards his last death; which stands with him at his open grave; which calls in his ear the summons to the judgement seat of an offended God; which scorches his face with the fires of hell and all in an atmosphere of fervor, aided by the entreaties of the sinner's friends, their prayers to God, their tears, the example of the repentance of other sinners.[41]

Clearly, this was evangelicalism in exemplary form. A Redemptorist Father likened the mission "to a thunder and lightning storm" which "bursts upon the scene with powerful sermons to arouse man from the lethargy of sin to a life of fervor."[42] With its emphasis on sin, its stress on fear of the Lord and its aim of arousing fear, reverence, awe, hatred of sin, and love of God, one can say, quite truthfully, that the parish mission was, indeed, a revival in all but name.

However, Catholic revivalism was different in its emphasis on turning away from the world and toward more celestial goals. Unlike Evangelical Protestantism which led to the evolution of the Protestant social gospel, with its emphasis on making the world into the Kingdom of God, Catholic evangelicalism removed the Catholic from the world and left him or her concerned mainly with achieving the after-life rather than attempting to improve the situation of his or her neighbor.

Another striking and critical difference of Catholic evangelicalism was the emphasis on the sacraments. By

itself, a personal decision for Christ was considered
incomplete. Conversion had to be verified by a "sacramental confession of one's sins and the eventual
reception of the Eucharist...."[43]

> ...for Catholics salvation was achieved through the
> instrumentality of the visible Church and its sacraments.
> The spirit of orthodoxy allowed for no other alternative.
> Catholic revivalism encouraged a sacramental evangel-
> icalism which not only urged the sinner to repent but also
> provided the means necessary for such a conversion. For
> Catholics personal conviction of sin was only the first step
> toward salvation and without the church the pursuit of
> holiness could not be realized.[44]

Even with the importance of the sacraments as the
bestowal of acceptance on the newly-confessed former
sinner, revivalism did give a special coloring to the
prevalent Tridentine Catholicism of the day. Catholic
evangelicalism was manifested in the heart not the
head; it spoke to the sinner's own personal life and
invited him or her to a personal experience of sin and
conversion.

The parish mission or revival soon became a common-
place event in the lives of Catholics and a major means of
evangelization. Great stress was placed on the importance of Church structures and institutions. The parish,
the key institution, was highlighted, the pastor was
supreme, and the congregations were "docile and obedient." Any growth of social involvement was impeded by
a "ghetto-mentality": Catholics against the world. The
pervasive presence of a very strong anti-Catholic senti-
ment during the latter half of the nineteenth century
was an important factor in this isolationism.

As parishes began to grow, both in size and number,
the decision as to when a mission should occur became

one for the pastor to make. Usually, missions took place every four or five years, since it was found that more frequent occurrences led to a too-routinized event with little novelty or success at engendering enthusiasm.

As with the Protestants, revivals soon became structured affairs, managed periods of grace called down by priests specifically trained and ladened with sermon notebooks suitable for a parish of any size, class or racial makeup.

Black Catholic Revivalism

Blacks were a part of the revival spirit in the Catholic Church from its very beginning. Present in the American Catholic Church from its birth, especially in the French and Spanish-settled areas of the country, the majority of Black Catholics in the seventeenth, eighteenth, and nineteenth centuries were found in Maryland and Louisiana, the slaves of Catholics, including Catholic clergy and religious.[45]

Little overt evangelization, beyond perfunctory instruction prior to baptism, was given to most of them. Yet Roman Catholicism was very attractive to many Blacks, especially those newly arrived from Africa, because of its seeming greater openness to the survival of traditional African beliefs and practices than Protestantism.

> In African religion there is a high God comparable to the Christian concept of a one God. But just as there are many spirits in Christianity, angels and saints, each especially empowered (St. Michael for strength, St. Raphael for healing), so, too in the African religion there are spirits for particular aspects of creation.[46]

This "similarity between the pantheon of gods and spirits in the African traditional religions and the saints of the Catholic Church" was certainly a factor in the acceptance by many Africans of the Roman Catholic faith.[47] Further rich context for inculturation was offered in other ways:

> The use of sacramentals (blessed objects), such as statues, pictures, candles, incense, holy water, rosaries, vestments, and relics, in Catholic ritual was more akin to the spirit of African piety than the coarseness of Puritan America; which held such objects to be idolatrous. Holy days, processions, Saints' feasts, days of fast and abstinence were all recognizable to the African who had observed the sacred days, festivals, and food taboos of his gods.[48]

On the other hand, many Blacks who were Catholic through no desire of their own did not care for it because of its inhibitions toward a more emotional experience of "church." "Prayer meetings, shouting and spirituals—the staples of Black Protestantism—were often foreign to the experience of Black Catholics" except at the parish missions.[49] While the Protestant faith denied the ritual use of sacred objects and devotion to the saints which were readily adaptable to African beliefs and theology, the formal structure of the Roman Rite did not permit the bodily participation and ecstatic behavior reminiscent of African patterns of dance and possession. Nor was the Bible or sermon as important in Catholic piety, an aspect of great importance to orally affective Africans.[50]

A further negative factor was the lack of an indigenous Black Catholic priesthood. It did not evolve because of the Catholic emphasis on years of training as a requirement for the priesthood and the overwhelming refusal of Catholic bishops and seminaries in the United

States to accept Black men for study for the priesthood. A major factor was the lack of acceptance of Blacks in Catholic seminaries. Only a very few Blacks were able to enter foreign seminaries. Thus, the status, authority, and influence of the Black Protestant minister was not duplicated among Black Catholics.[51]

However, for the many Blacks who were Catholic, the Catholic parish mission became a sought after and welcome source of renewal and revival. These missions were at first integrated, but the Blacks usually sat in the galleries of the churches. Soon, segregated Black parishes began to emerge and with them evolved an apostolate for the evangelization of Black America. Coupled with this was the trend toward a revival being held for one particular parish. As a result, revivals ceased to be interracial gatherings and revivalists simply included the Black parish in their itinerary.

Although the Church still made no special effort to evangelize Blacks who were not Catholic, it did encourage the use of a revival as "a particularly effective way of evangelizing the Black population" because it provided "a more vigorous stimulus,"[52] thus unknowingly recognizing the African desire for a more emotive religious experience.

The Black Catholic was exposed to the fervent exhortation and the spirit-filled conversion experience of revivals in two ways. He or she either attended a mission within the parish, or stole away to the meetings of the Black Protestant Church. Regardless of the source, however, even after revivalism began to wane, the seed had been sown from which would emerge the Black Catholic movement of the twentieth century which, in turn, has led to the development of a distinctly Black form of Catholic worship, the Black Catholic Congress movement, and the emergence of a Black

Catholic Theology (these will be discussed in Chapter Eight).

Notes

1. Much of the material for this chapter is based upon Hayes, "Black Catholic Revivalism."

2. Anthony Walton, "Patriots," in *Lure and Loathing: Essays on Race, Identity, and the Ambivalence of Assimilation*, ed. by Gerald Early (N.Y.: Penguin Books, 1993), p. 260.

3. An in-depth discussion of Christianity and the issue of race can be found in the previously cited work by Forrest G. Wood, *The Arrogance of Race*.

4. William G. McLoughlin, *Revivals, Awakenings and Reform: An Essay on Religion and Social Change in America, 1607-1977* (Chicago: University of Chicago Press, 1978), p. 2.

5. Ibid.

6. Success through hard work is seen as a person's duty and responsibility, a perspective which still negatively influences perceptions of the poor and unemployed in the United States today. Coining of the phrase is attributed to Max Weber, sociologist of religion, who, in turn, attributes the dissemination of this ideology to the teachings of Jean Calvin and his followers. See Weber's *The Protestant Ethic and the Spirit of Capitalism*.

7. Ibid., p. 59.

8. Bernard A. Weisenberger, *They Gathered at the River: The Story of the Great Revivalists and Their Impact Upon Religion in America* (Chicago: Quadrangle Books, 1966) p. 28.

9. Ibid., p. 21.

10. Ibid., p. 27.

11. Ibid., p. 39.

12. Ibid., p. 86.

13. Charles G. Finney, "What a Revival of Religion Is," *Lecture on Revivals of Religion* (Cambridge: Belknap Press of Harvard University Press, 1960), p. 12.

14. Ibid., p. 13.

15. Ibid., p. 4.

16. Weisberger, *They Gathered at the River*, p. 144.

17. Albert J. Raboteau, *Slave Religion: The "Invisible" Institution in the Antebellum South* (New York: Oxford University Press, 1978), p. 148.

18. Milton C. Sernett, *Black Religion and American Evangelicalism: White Protestants, Plantation Missions and the Flowering of Negro Christianity 1787-1865*, ATLA Monograph Series, No. 7 (Metuchen, N.J.: Scarecrow Press and the American Theological Library Association, 1975), p. 25.

19. Ibid., p. 59.

20. In Virginia, a law of 1667, as noted by Lerone Bennett, decreed that "The conferring of baptisme doth not alter the condition of the person as to his bondage or freedom." Other colonies soon followed suit. See *Before the Mayflower: A History of Black America* (N.Y.: Penguin Books, 1993, Sixth revised and updated ed.).

20a. See Winthrop D. Jordan, *White Over Black: American Attitudes Toward the Negro*, 1550–1812 (Baltimore: Penguin Books, 1968).

21. See Wood, ch. 4, pp. 126ff.

22. Ibid., p. 54.

23. Ibid., p. 62.

24. Timothy L. Smith, "Slavery and Theology: The Emergence of Black Christian Consciousness in Nineteenth Century America," *Church History* 41 (1972), pp. 497-498. This does not mean, however, that there were not those slaves who did passively accept what they were told without questioning it.

25. Luther P. Jackson, "Religious Instruction of Negroes, 1830 to 1860, with Special Reference to South Carolina," *Journal of Negro History* 15 (January 1930), p. 72.

26. Sernett, *Black Religion and American Evangelicalism*.

27. Ibid., p. 84. An interesting question which calls for further research is how many of the Africans brought to the Eastern English-speaking colonies were Muslim or even Christian, the latter converted in Africa by the French and Portuguese who first explored and exploited the land and peoples of West Africa. A fictional account of the impact and clash of both Islam and Christianity with the traditional religions of the peoples of the West coast can be found in the novels of Maryse Conde, *Segu* (New York: Ballantine Books, 1988) and *The Children of Segu* (New York: Ballantine Books, 1990).

28. See "From the Confessions of Nat Turner," in Mullane, *Crossing Danger Water*, pp. 88-97 as well as Bennett, *Before the Mayflower*, Franklin, *From Slavery to Freedom*, and others on the history of this period.

29. See Raboteau, *Slave Religion*, ch. 5.

30. Cone, *My Soul Looks Back* (Nashville: Abingdon Press, 1982, Journeys of Faith series, Robert A. Raines, ed., republished Maryknoll: Orbis Books, 1986), p. 24.

31. Smith, "Slavery and Theology," p. 502.

32. Ibid., p. 504.

33. Ibid., p. 506.

34. Olin P. Moyd, "The Old-Time Revival," *Freeing the Spirit* II (Summer 1973), p. 23.

35. Jay P. Dolan, *Catholic Revivalism: The American Experience, 1830-1900* (Notre Dame: Notre Dame Press, 1978), p. xv.

36. Dolan, *Catholic Revivalism*, p. xv.

37. Maryland was the only Catholic colony. However, it was founded on the basis of religious freedom of choice—a freedom short-lived, however, as the ensuing Protestant majority soon outlawed the practice of Catholicism. See Dolan, *The American Catholic Experience* (Garden City, N.Y.: Doubleday and Co., 1985), ch. 3.

38. Ibid., p. 9.

39. Ibid., p. 86.

40. Jay P. Dolan, "American Catholics and Revival Religion, 1850-1900," *Horizons* 3 (Spring 1976), p. 44.

41. Ibid., p. 46.

42. Ibid., p. 45.

43. Ibid., p. 54.

44. Ibid.

45. For example, the Jesuits had African slaves working on their four plantations in Maryland from the end of the seventeenth century until 1837 when they were sold to Louisiana. Many other religious orders, male and female, also held slaves, and it was a common custom for young women entering the convent to bring a slave as part of their dowry. See Davis, *Black Catholics*, pp. 36-37.

46. Clarence Joseph Rivers, *The Spirit in Worship* (Cincinnati, Ohio: Stimuli, Inc., 1978), p. 4.

47. As Woods notes: "In reality, the hybridization of the church was, despite the apprehensions of some Catholic officials, fully in accord with Pope Gregory XV's injunction, on founding the Sacred Congregation for the Propagation of the Faith," that the missionary fathers should "do their utmost to adapt themselves to the native customs" and "avoid imposing European culture on converts" (pp. 7-8, *Arrogance*); an admonition, sadly, too often observed in the breaching of it in the Americas and Africa.

48. Raboteau, *Slave Religion,* p. 87.

49. Ibid., p. 272.

50. Ibid. For a fuller discussion of the similarities and differences, especially in terms of the African understanding of "spirit possession" and the African American conceptualization of the working of the Spirit, see Diana L. Hayes, "Slain in the Spirit: Black Americans and the Holy Spirit," in *The Journal of the Interdenominational Theological Center*, Vol. XX (#1/2, Fall 1992/Spring 1993), pp. 97-115.

51. The first Black Catholic priest ordained in the United States was Fr. Augustus Tolton in 1886. Today there are only approximately 300+ Black priests and religious in the United States. See Davis, *Black Catholics*, pp. 145-162, and Stephen Ochs, *Desegregating the Altar: The Josephites and the Struggle for Black Priests, 1871-1960* (Baton Rouge: Louisiana State University Press, 1990).

52. Dolan, *Catholic Revivalism*, p. 115.

3

The Emergence
of a Black
Liberation Theology

The intermeshing of the various streams
discussed in Chapters One and Two led to the emergence
of a systematically developed, consciously articulated,
and contextually based Black Theology of Liberation in
the late 1960s.[1]

James Cone, considered the first to articulate a Black
Theology,[2] speaks of three major catalysts for the
development of Black Liberation Theology in the 1960s:
the Civil Rights Movement, the Black Power Movement
and the influence of Malcolm X on the Black Nationalist
Movement, and the reaction to the negative depiction of
Black religion set forth in Joseph Washington's *Black
Religion*.[3]

Cone also acknowledges, as does Dwight Hopkins[4] and
other Black theologians, the importance of the publication of the "Black Power Statement"[5] of the National
Conference of Negro Churchmen[6] as well as the founding
of the Society for the Study of Black Religion (1970) in
"initiating" the development of a theological consciousness that separated radical Black Christianity from the
more passive religious expression of the mainline white

churches.[7] In addition, however, Hopkins stresses the influence of the early slave narratives, as noted in Chapter One, seeing them as the primordial voice of Black Liberation Theology, its first "stumbling and stammering" tongue.[8]

Another way of viewing the development of Black Theology is in the three stages presented by Gayraud Wilmore. The first stage, from July 31, 1966 to July 4, 1970 covers the period of the publication of the above-mentioned "Black Power Statement" and culminates with "The Black Declaration of Independence" of the NCBC. This period is one of movement from the passive disobedience of the Civil Rights movement to the provocative assertiveness of the Black Power movement. The second stage saw a turn toward the academic world and the greater involvement of seminary professors as opposed to the radical Black ministers, many in white Churches, who were active in the first stage. It is at this stage that Black Theology began to be defined clearly and presented in a more systematic way in response to the continuing demand of Black seminarians and theological students (beginning in 1969) and to the growing need and desire for a methodological articulation of Black Theology. This period saw the founding of the Society for the Study of Black Religion (SSBR) "to engage in scholarly research and discussion about the religious experiences [and] to encourage the teaching and discussion of the Black religious experience in the curricula of college and seminary departments of religion and theological seminaries in the U.S. and elsewhere."[9]

However, the turn to academia resulted in Black Theology's becoming disconnected from its source, the Black community and Church—the Black experience *in toto*. With its growing establishment as an academic discipline, its discussions became increasingly abstract and lifeless; they, to a certain extent, established Black Theology's academic credentials but at the risk of losing its contextual relevance and liberative force. This period, from 1970 to approximately 1975, led to the third and present stage in which Black Theology has attempted to return to the Black community itself, especially the Black Church, and to widen its focus to recognize the global connectedness of oppressed peoples throughout the world. The context of oppression has widened to include sexism and classism as well as racism and to begin renewing the ties and dialogue among Black Churches across denominational lines.[10]

In the remainder of this chapter, I will discuss this history in greater detail as a source for Black Theology's emergence.

The Civil Rights Movement

The Civil Rights Movement with its call for the "true integration" of African Americans into the mainstream of life in the United States and thus the necessary elimination of the "Jim Crow"[11] laws which supported and enabled segregation and the second-class treatment of Blacks caused a dramatic raising of consciousness among both Blacks and whites. This Christian non-violent movement particularly affected young black ministers (at this time, predominantly male[12]) who were confronted, over and over again in their ministry, by the paradox of preaching about a Christianity seemingly at odds with the best interests of their own people. The dichotomy they saw and experienced in what was preached by the Christian churches in the United States and in what was actually practiced by American Christians, especially those who were white, led to serious soul-searching on their part. Cone reflected upon this in his autobiographical work, *My Soul Looks Back*:

> ...I became more confused about the relationship between the Christian gospel and social justice...White churches, almost without exception, were adamant in rejecting integration in churches, schools, and social gatherings. Black churches, however, were equally determined on the other side of the issue. How could both black and white churches be Christian if they took opposite stands and both claimed Christ and the Bible as the basis of their views?[13]

The growing disillusionment of African Americans of their own age with both the Civil Rights Movement and with Christianity itself served as a further goad to their consciences, leading them toward a greater understanding of and allegiance toward the developing Black Power Movement.

Black Christian theologians sought to discern how Christianity could be taught in a way which was in keeping with the teachings of Christ yet which would also lay open the hypocrisy of the major proponents of that teaching for so many centuries. They questioned whether Blacks could continue to profess faith in a God who apparently was not with them but was on the side only of those who sought to continue the oppression of Black people throughout the world.[14] Howard Thurman had eloquently phrased the question that was agonizing many Black Christians at this time many years earlier:

> Why is it that Christianity seems impotent to deal radically and therefore effectively, with the issues of discrimination and injustice on the basis of race, religion, and national origin? Is this impotency due to a betrayal of the genius of the religion, or is it due to a basic weakness in the religion itself?[15]

Black Christians of the 1960s found themselves with a faith that had sustained them for centuries through the horrors of slavery and segregation but which was becoming increasingly impossible to defend because they had little or no memory of its connection to their lives. They had little understanding of the hard-fought-for foundation of that faith, of its history, or of how it had been forged in the fires of slavery, for, by the 1960s, their faith had become, all too often, something to which they were simply accustomed. They no longer had to fight to preserve and maintain it. It was no longer a truly lived faith but had become one simply held on to because it had always been so.

The Civil Rights Movement began in the mid-1950s. Although there were a number of different catalysts, most historians agree that it was the refusal of Mrs. Rosa Parks of Montgomery, Alabama to give up her bus seat to a white man in 1956 that was the immediate spark.[16] The movement began within the historically Black Churches from which it obtained its leaders and supporters, but it was also a grassroots movement which found its strength in the people themselves.

> If it hadn't been for Ella Baker, there wouldn't have been any SNCC (Student Nonviolent Coordinating Committee). When you looked at Sunflower County Mississippi, you had to look at Fannie Lou Hamer.... When you are talking about important roles, you have to ask which person has the most important role—the one who speaks or the one who got the people there?[17]

It was with the founding of the Southern Christian Leadership Conference with Dr. Martin Luther King, Jr. at its head as the movement's most prominent spokesman that the push for concrete changes in American society began to take shape. King sought to relate the

Christian gospel to the struggle for justice of blacks in America. He was influenced in his theology and in his praxis by the non-violent philosophy of Mahatma Gandhi and the Social Gospel emphasis of the Protestant Church which mandated a role for the Church in the betterment of society and human life.[18]

He was also influenced deeply by the exposition of the natural law by Sts. Augustine and Aquinas as can be seen most clearly in his "Letter from Birmingham Jail":

> One may well ask, 'How can you advocate breaking some laws and obeying others?' The answer is found in the fact that there are two types of laws: there are *just* and there are *unjust* laws. I would agree with Saint Augustine that 'an unjust law is no law at all.'
>
> Now what is the difference between the two? How does one determine when a law is just or unjust? A just law is a man-made code that squares with the moral law or the law of God. An unjust law is a code that is out of harmony with the moral law. To put it in the terms of Saint Thomas Aquinas, an unjust law is a human law that is not rooted in eternal and natural law. Any law that degrades human personality is unjust...segregation is not only politically, economically and sociologically unsound, but it is morally wrong and sinful.... I can urge men to disobey segregation ordinances because they are morally wrong.[19]

However, the greatest influence on his theology of "the beloved community" made up of "neighbors," both Black and white who cared for and loved each other, was his own context as the descendant of a line of Black Baptist ministers born and raised in the segregated South.[20]

Most white churches and their theologians, as well as many Blacks, rejected King's approach initially, asserting that religion and politics could not and should not mix. Jesus and the Church were seen as above culture (society) or in conflict with it rather than as a part of and an active force within that culture and, therefore, within history itself. The movement, thus, initially received little theological or financial support from the mainline denominational Churches, Black or white. This was, however, a blessing of sorts, because it provided the activists in the movement with the freedom to discern for themselves what their goals and objectives were without undue influence from naysayers, foot-draggers and co-opters of their message.

The Civil Rights Movement began as a grassroots movement in the South with ordinary people, students, homemakers, day laborers, domestics, and others as its foundation and strength. As the sit-ins and marches began to take on a shape and cohesiveness of their own, many Black ministers, most of whom were young and just recently out of the seminary, called upon their own and their parishioners' experiences in the South to give them strength and courage. The old spirituals, coupled with new freedom songs often made up as they went along (as the spirituals themselves were created), provided new understandings of their foreparents' earlier struggles against captivity. The old stories and the history of Blacks in the United States, a history often overlooked and nearly forgotten by most, were revived as they sought support from the past and encouragement for their efforts in the present.

The lives and struggles of the founders of the first independent Black Churches, Richard Allen (AME), James Varick (AMEZ) and others, were rediscovered and made available; the sermons and other writings of these and others such as Henry Highland Garnett, who urged the slaves to take their freedom into their own hands, of Nat Turner, who turned those words into bloody reality, and of Henry McNeale Turner, who strove for Black self-affirmation, were brought out and held up as examples of the unending Black struggle for liberty and justice and the importance of their Christian faith in their efforts to attain these goals.[21]

The historically liberating role which the Black Churches had originally played in the lives of their people, as related in Chapters 1 and 2, were slowly revived. For, sadly, by the middle of the twentieth century, many of these Churches had lost sight of their revolutionary beginnings. They no longer resembled those Churches whose birth had been the first difficult step toward true freedom of body and spirit by and for Blacks. Instead, they now too often mouthed the same pieties which they had adopted wholesale from the Euro-American theology in which their ministers had been trained—a training which, too often, led to the further dichotomization of the goals of actual freedom for their race from the life and words of Jesus Christ because it separated them from their own history and experience.

African American youth were also mobilized in the Civil Rights Movement and served as the "foot soldiers" who prodded both ministers and laity into greater involvement. As members of the Student Nonviolent Coordinating Committee (SNCC), they, along with white students, scoured the South running voter registration drives and "sitting, lying, riding, and praying-in" at segregated lunch counters, bus stations, churches, jails, and city halls to garner the nation's attention.[22]

Despite the many gains of the Civil Rights Movement, however, there was still often little solace to be found within the Black Churches, many of which still refused to support King, including his own National Baptist Convention from which he and others eventually broke to form the Progressive Baptist Convention, Inc., seeing him only as a radical and trouble-maker. They had become complacent and set in their ways, especially the mainline Churches. The struggle for freedom was increasingly being seen by young Blacks as a political rather than religious struggle, while the Black Church and Christianity in general were seen as parasites draining life from the Black community. The stage was set for the emergence of young Black nationalists who had no room in their political agenda for a God of any kind. Rather, they saw human action and effort alone as the only means of bringing about viable change, especially, in the inner cities of the North. They sought power for Blacks to counter the power they correctly believed was held by the white majority political and economic structures of the United States while questioning, at the same time, the need for Blacks to become a part of those structures.

Their actions further decimated belief in the ability of the Black Church to cause constructive change in American society as they critiqued the efforts of King and his followers as simply attempts to be accepted by and allowed to assimilate into the predominant society, thereby forsaking the distinctiveness of Black culture, history, and tradition. Stokely Carmichael, who first raised the call for Black Power,[23] argued that "...integration is a subterfuge for the maintenance of white supremacy" which "assumes that (whites have) something which Blacks want or should want, as if being close to white people enhances the humanity of Blacks."[24]

The continued intransigence of the "dominant" white culture, which was especially exposed when King shifted his efforts, unsuccessfully, to the allegedly integrated and more liberal northern urban cities, helped to win converts to the call for "Black Power" as many young Blacks began to question the continued viability of a non-violent movement in arenas that were becoming increasingly violent. As a result, the non-violent movement which had brought significant change to the South with the abolishing of many of the "Jim Crow" laws was slowly but inexorably pushed to the sidelines by the revolutionary rhetoric of the Black Power movement. The cry was for the achievement of freedom by whatever means necessary as bowed heads gave way to clenched and upraised fists.[25]

The Black Power Movement

The Black Power Movement was the cauldron from which all of the unrest, dissatisfaction, and frustration that had been simmering for so long among African Americans finally boiled over. It was a movement born of "long, hot summers" of violence and the slogan "burn, baby, burn."[26] It was the result of a slowly dawning recognition by many young Blacks that "peace, love and reconciliation" were not working and were not going to work. They argued that in order for Blacks to gain their freedom, it would have to be wrested from the unwilling hands of the oppressor. Thus, the cry for Black Power can be seen as "an expression of the need for Black authenticity in a white-dominated society..."[27]

A sense of pride in being Black, in being different from the white mainstream, began to emerge. With this feeling came the realization, already articulated by Carmichael, that integration was meant to be only on the white man's terms.

While King and his Christian activists were engaged in their efforts to open the eyes and convert the hearts of white America, another voice, that of Malcolm X,[28] was being raised in the North. Malcolm, the provocatively eloquent spokesman for the Nation of Islam[29] (also known as the Black Muslims), counseled a more activist approach. He declared, unequivocally, the need for Blacks to stand up and take positive steps toward their liberation and enfranchisement and against the persistent racist assaults against their humanity, calling for recognition that Blacks must inevitably choose between the "ballot" or the "bullet" if they were to not only survive but attain meaningful power within the United States.[30]

Initially, at opposite ends of the political and religious spectrum with Martin Luther King, Jr. and appealing to different audiences, King to Southern rural Blacks and Malcolm X to Northern urban Blacks, as Malcolm became disillusioned with the teachings and behavior of the Nation's leader, The Honorable Elijah Muhammad, he began to move closer to an understanding of the value and legitimacy of all humanity regardless of race or creed. At the same time, after his harsh encounter with Northern racism and intransigence, King was beginning to realize the connections between racism, politics and the economic situation of Black Americans, a connection which Malcolm X had sought consistently to expose.

James Cone, in *Martin and Malcolm and America*, presents the thesis that both King and Malcolm X were moving closer together in their understanding of the way in which Blacks were treated in the United States and the interconnection of racial and economic oppression.[31]

Malcolm, who began his political and religious life preaching that whites were "devils," began to see himself as complementing King in certain ways while, at the same time, serving as a focal point for the growing Black Nationalism Movement. In a speech in Harlem where he shared the stage with Mrs. Fanny Lou Hamer, the tireless civil rights worker from Sunflower County, Mississippi, Malcolm noted

So I say, in my conclusion, as Mrs. Hamer pointed out, the brothers and sisters in Mississippi are being beaten and killed for no reason other than they want to be treated as first-class citizens. There's only one way to be a first-class citizen. There's only one way to be independent. There's only one way to be free. It's not something that someone gives to you. It's something that you take. Nobody can give you independence. Nobody can give you equality of justice or anything. If you're a man, you take it. If you can't take it, you don't deserve it.[32]

His words were remarkably similar to those written by King as he lay incarcerated in the Birmingham City Jail in 1963: "We know through painful experience that freedom is never voluntarily given by the oppressor; it must be demanded by the oppressed."[33]

The call for Black Power at first stunned and then, paradoxically, revitalized the discourse and praxis of many young African American Christians. At this critical juncture, a group of young Black men, theologically trained but with a hunger to understand who they were, where they had come from and why they were and remained Christian, stepped out onto the stage of history.

Refusing to relinquish their Christian heritage, they, however, raised critical questions about their faith:

If God is the Creator of all persons and through Christ has made salvation possible for every one, why are some oppressed and segregated in the churches and in society on the basis of color? How can whites claim Christian identity which emphasizes the love and justice of God, and still support and tolerate the injustice committed against blacks by churches and society? Why do blacks accept white interpretations of Christianity that deny their humanity and ignore their own encounter of God (extending back to Africa) as the liberator and protector of black victims of oppression?[34]

Rather than denounce Black Power, however, as many entreated them to do, these young Black Christians empathized with and understood the reasons behind the violence and unrest taking place in the ghettos. But, at the same time, they realized they could not condone it uncritically. They, therefore, came together with other activist Black clergy and scholars to form the National Conference of Negro Churchmen and, in 1966, issued a ground-breaking statement on Black Power which set the tone for the ensuing debate on the role of religion in the political liberation of a people and the stage for Black Theology's emergence.[35]

Addressed to the leaders of America, white clergy, Black citizens, and the mass media, the statement acknowledged and asserted the need of Black people for power in the United States:

> The fundamental distortion facing us in the controversy about "black power" is rooted in a gross imbalance of power and conscience between Negroes and white Americans. It is this distortion, mainly, which is responsible for the widespread, though often inarticulate, assumption that white people are justified in getting what they want through the use of power, but that Negro Americans must either by nature or by circumstance, make their appeal only through conscience. As a result, the power of white men and the conscience of black men have both been corrupted. The power of white men is corrupted because it meets little meaningful resistance from Negroes to temper it and keep white men from aping God. The conscience of black men is corrupted because, having no power to implement the demands of conscience, the concern for justice is transmuted into a distorted form of love which, in the absence of justice, becomes chaotic self-surrender. Powerlessness breeds a race of beggars. We are faced now with a situation where conscienceless power meets powerless conscience.[36]

They also recognized that Black Power alone was unable and unwilling to answer the questions they had raised regarding God and his actions. Instead, that movement became increasingly identified with a Black nationalism that too often at its foundations rejected both God and country, a step many Blacks were unwilling to take. For there were still many who felt that the Black Church and Christianity still had something positive to offer to the struggle for justice in the United States. The resulting polarization pushed many of these radical Black ministers, who could not relinquish their love of Christ for hatred of part of God's creation, into looking at the meaning of their love and faith with newly opened eyes. They looked beyond Black Church history to the history of Black people throughout their sojourn in the United States, a history in which both the religious and secular worlds had always been intertwined, a result, they came to understand, of their African ancestry where the dualistic separation of the sacred and the secular did not exist.

They sought to invalidate white and Black assumptions that Blacks had brought nothing with them and had contributed nothing while they were here, revealing instead the deep religiosity and sense of the sacred which had pervaded African lives and were passed on and retained by African Americans.[37] They pointed to the slaves' reinterpretation of the life, death and resurrection of Jesus Christ and their "new-old" vision of the Church as exemplified in the richness of their life of worship, in the depth and spirituality of Black music, both religious and secular, and in the invincible strength arising out of their faith which enabled their people to "keep on keeping on," despite chains, whips, lynchings, hunger, miseducation, fear, and poverty and the teaching of a distorted Christianity to an illiterate and captive people.[38]

The Publication of Black Religion

In the midst of all this, Joseph Washington's book, *Black Religion*, was published. Although Washington, himself Black, agreed that there was a unique Black culture which had developed a distinctive Black religion, he saw this as cause for condemnation and concern rather than for pride and joy. Washington asserted that

> Negro congregations are not churches but religious societies—religion can choose to worship whatever gods are pleasing. But a church without a theology, the interpretation of and response to the will of God for the faithful, is a contradiction in terms.[39]

For Washington, Blacks had only a folk religion and a "folk" culture.[40] The only true religion, he argued, was that of white Christians who had, however, failed to successfully integrate Black Christians into their churches, thus leading to the sad state of Black religion. Washington, further, contended that Black religion was not a faith but an ideology because it lacked a "true" Christian theology which could be found only in white Christian Churches. He argued, in company with many white theologians at that time,[41] that the Christian gospel has nothing to do with the Black struggle for freedom and justice in American society, an argument which attacked the foundational premise of Black and all other liberation theologies.

Black Religion was welcomed by some theologians as a needed indictment of Christianity which reminded both Blacks and whites of the dangers presented to Christianity in the United States by divisions along the "color bar." It was recognized that segregation had indeed isolated Negro religion "from the life-giving stream of theological discussion and growth."[42] At the same time, many critiqued the book as too simplistic and naive in its theological and historical interpretations.[43] The reduction of religion to an ideology "functional in design and utilitarian in purpose" merely because its prime concern was for freedom and justice in the here and now was also seen as indefensibly restrictive of the true meaning of religion.[44]

Other Black scholars argued that "a people's Christian identity didn't depend upon its intellectual ability to engage in...theoretical discussions...."[45] Blacks had spent most of their lives merely attempting to stay alive and to provide sustenance and a viable future for their descendants. For that reason, they acknowledged that much of their religion could, in one sense, be considered an opiate promising "pie in the sky when you die." But it was also a sustaining force which gave them reason to hope for redemption in the here and now. There was no felt need for an articulated theology to define the meaning of Christ or God; that meaning was assimilated quite simply and clearly expressed in their preaching and in their songs of faith. Christ was the Liberator, the Savior, the One to whom you could turn when all else had failed or everything and everyone was against you. God was the Creator Father, opponent of evil and source of joy. This simple theology was enough to hold families together and to make life worth living. This tension, between passivity and radicalism, is, as noted earlier, one of the marks of Black religion in the United States. Gayraud Wilmore sees it as a tension necessary for the maintenance both of the people's faith and of their very survival.[46]

It is only today, as the more blatant and obvious expression of racism in the United States has been replaced by subtler and more insidious forms, that African Americans, as a religious people, have begun to see the need for a more systematic articulation of the faith and hope which is theirs. They began to realize that the time had come to express not only to themselves but to the world at large what it meant to be both Black and Christian.

Washington's position was untenable for several reasons. First, it failed to recognize that faith is more than just theology. It is also worship and social expression. Faith is the lived out expression of a people's hope and belief in someone or something greater than themselves. It was this faith that had nurtured Blacks from their first contact with Christianity and had kept them alive throughout the travails of their life's journey.[47]

Second, if religion has nothing to do with freedom and justice, as Washington claimed, then most of the major Christian denominations as well as their source, Judaism, could also be seen merely as "folk" religions as well. For it can be argued that Judaism also arose from the particular context of an oppressed people who reflected on God's activity in their lives and engaged in dialogue on the meaning of that activity for them, leading to the development of a theology which arose from their faith and their efforts to understand it. The fact that one people had an oral tradition (both Blacks and originally Hebrews) and another a written tradition (which, however, did not evolve until much later) is, essentially, of no relevance; each are equally valid.

Third, those white churches which were equally untheological in their thought and socially oriented in their praxis and religious expression were ignored by Washington. Yet, one could argue that their weaknesses are even more telling because they are not now nor have they ever been artificially separated from their white brethren, as have been the Black Churches.

Washington presented a bias which was common at the time, namely, that nothing of value could be found in the Black setting. He saw Christianity as defined by whites as the better way, despite the obvious dichotomy between their preaching and their praxis because it was the white and therefore the right way.[48]

His importance, however, lies in his challenge to Black Christians to speak out and to articulate an apologetical theology which was expressive of their faith. *Black Religion* served as a catalyst for further reflection on the meaning and relevance of Christianity for African Americans. At the same time, it presented an argument which many felt ridiculed Black faith and encouraged the "white man's way" as the only way. Thus, it inadvertently helped to further divide the Black community between those who sought equality through integration, at a moderate and accommodating pace, and those who were beginning to call impatiently for more overt and radical action, including separation of the races if necessary.

Many Black Christian ministers, as noted above, found themselves caught in the middle. They were tired of going slowly but were not ready to completely sever themselves from their native land or their native religion, although some eventually did both.[49] Angered by the assertions of Washington that their churches and beliefs were the mere fantasies of an illiterate and non-intellectual people, they sought to rebut his arguments with their own, in an effort to prove that the religious faith of Black people was not only Christian but was, in actuality, the only true form of Christianity being practiced in the United States.

It is from this context that Black Theology emerged: the Civil Rights Movement as articulated and led by Dr. Martin Luther King, Jr., the Black Nationalism of Malcolm X and the Black Power Movement, and the critical evaluation and condemnation of Black religion by Joseph Washington and the rebuttal of his thesis by other

Black theologians. Black Theology was the result of an effort to interpret in language that spoke to Black people themselves of "God's liberating presence in a society where Blacks were being economically exploited and politically marginalized because of their skin color."[50] It was meant to serve as a "theological witness" which rejected racism and affirmed that the Black struggle for freedom was not only consistent with Christ's gospel but also that it was the proclamation of that gospel. It was a theological response to crisis: riots, non-violence overcome by violence, Black Power rhetoric, and Black and white condemnation.

Notes

1. It should be noted that Black Liberation Theology and Latin American Liberation Theology emerged at approximately the same time but independently of each other in their respective countries.

2. His first work, *Black Theology and Black Power* (N.Y.: Seabury Press, 1969; reprint 1986; 20th Anniversary ed., N.Y.: Harper & Row, 1989), was a scathing critique of the hypocrisy of white Christianity and set the context for Black Theology in the experience of Black Americans. His other works include *A Black Theology of Liberation* (Philadelphia: Lippincott, 1970, reprint 1986; 20th Anniversary ed., Maryknoll, N.Y.: Orbis, 1990); *The Spirituals and the Blues* (N.Y.: Seabury Press, 1972, reprint 1991, Maryknoll, N.Y.: Orbis); *God of the Oppressed* (N.Y.: Seabury Press, 1975); *My Soul Looks Back* (Nashville: Abingdon Press, 1982; Maryknoll, N.Y.: Orbis, 1986); *For My People: Black Theology and the Black Church* (Maryknoll, N.Y.: Orbis Books, 1984); *Speaking the Truth: Ecumenism, Liberation and Black Theology* (Grand Rapids, MI:Eerdmans, 1986), and *Martin, Malcolm and America: A Dream or A Nightmare* (Maryknoll, N.Y.: Orbis, 1992) and countless articles.

3. *Black Religion: The Negro and Christianity in the United States* (Boston: Beacon Press, 1964).

4. Hopkins is the author of *Black Theology: United States and South Africa* (Maryknoll, NY: Orbis, 1984) and the previously cited, *Shoes That Fit Our Feet*, and, with George Cummings, is editor of *Cut Loose Your Stammering Tongues*.

5. See James Cone and Gayraud Wilmore, eds. *Black Theology: A Documentary History*, Vol. One: 1966-1979 (Maryknoll, N.Y.: Orbis, 2nd ed. rev., 1993), pp. 19-27.

6. This became the National Conference of Black Christians and is no longer active.

7. See *For My People*, p. 1, the "General Introduction" to *Black Theology*, Vol. 1, pp. 1-11 and "Introduction" in Hopkins and Cummings, eds., *Cut Loose*, pp. ix-xxiii.

8. James Evans in his recent work, *We Have Been Believers: An African American Systematic Theology* (Minneapolis: Fortress Press, 1993), also discusses the importance of the slave narratives and their influence on the formulation of a Black religious consciousness.

9. By-laws of the SSBR, Article 1, section 2; also see Cone, *For My People*, ch. 1, pp. 25-28.

10. Much of this section is based on "The Origins of Black Theology," chapter 1 of *For My People*. The entire book and its footnotes are a valuable source of further background on the first fifteen years of Black Theology in the United States.

11. See definition in Chapter One.

12. See Chapter Six for a discussion of the continuing development of Black Theology in the form of Womanist Theology.

13. Cf. p. 27.

14. William R. Jones addresses this issue in his work, *Is God a White Racist?: A Preamble to Black Theology* (N.Y.: Anchor Doubleday, 1973), arguing that there was little evidence that God had ever supported African Americans in their struggle for equality, and that until they could present such evidence, the only response was that God was both white and racist. Jones, a Unitarian Universalist minister, also called upon the Black Churches, as we shall see in Chapter Four, to adopt a human-centered rather than a Christocentric faith in order to resolve the question of theodicy, God's role in human suffering.

15. Howard Thurman, *Jesus and the Disinherited* (Richmond, IN: Friends Press, 1981, originally published by Abingdon Press in 1949), p. 7. Although many Christians, both then and now, would argue that the fault lies with humanity's betrayal, others see the deficiency with Christianity itself. See Forrest G. Wood, *The Arrogance of Faith.* From the perspective of an historian rather than a theologian, Wood asserts that "Christianity, in the five centuries since its message was first carried to the peoples of the New World—and, in particular, to the natives and transplanted Africans of English North America and the United States—has been fundamentally racist in its ideology, organization, and practice (p. xviii, Preface).

16. The Black citizens of Montgomery had been in search of someone who would serve as a viable defendant in a legal action challenging the constitutionality of the segregated bus system in their city. Mrs. Parks, an active NAACP member, was aware of this but, at the same time, did not set out to become that person. Rather, as she has often stated, that day she was simply "tired" after a long day of work. See Taylor Branch, *Parting the Waters: America in the King Years, 1954-1963* (New York: Simon and Schuster, 1988), for a full discussion of the boycott.

17. Hollis Watkins talk, Southern Conference Organizing Committee meeting, Birmingham, Ala., December 2, 1989, as cited in Kay Mills, *This Little Light of Mine: The Life of Fannie Lou Hamer* (New York: Dutton, 1993), p. 202.

18. See discussion in Chapter Two on the Social Gospel.

19. Martin Luther King, Jr., *A Testament of Hope: The Essential Writings of Martin Luther King, Jr.*, James M. Washington, ed. (N.Y.: Harper and Row, 1986), p. 293.

20. See Lewis Baldwin, *There Is a Balm in Gilead: The Cultural Roots of Martin Luther King, Jr.* (Minneapolis: Fortress, 1991) and *To Make The Wounded Whole: The Cultural Legacy of Martin Luther King, Jr.* (Minneapolis: Fortress Press, 1992), and James Cone, *Martin, Malcolm and America: A Dream or a Nightmare.* King, during his brief lifetime, set forth his theology in several works: *Stride Toward Freedom: The Montgomery Story* (1958, republished San Francisco: Harper San Francisco, 1987), *The Strength To Love* (1963, republished Minneapolis: Augsburg Fortress, 1981), *Why We Can't Wait* (1964, republished N.Y.: NAL 1993), *Where Do We Go From Here: Chaos or Community?* (Boston: Beacon Press, 1967) and *The Trumpet of Conscience* (1967, republished San Francisco: Harper San Francisco, 1989). The first and second volumes of his collected papers have recently been published; see Clayborne Carson et al., eds., *The Papers of Martin Luther King, Jr* (University of California Press, Vol. 1, 1994, Vol. 2, 1995).

21. See Chapter 1, footnotes 20 and 23.

22. See Clayborne Carson, *In Struggle: SNCC and the Black Awakening of the 1960's* (Cambridge: Harvard University Press, 1981, and Taylor Branch, *Parting the Waters.*

23. See Stokely Carmichael and Charles Hamilton, *Black Power*. Once a leader in SNCC, Carmichael and Willie Ricks, another SNCC leader, raised the cry for "Black Power" on the Meredith march from Memphis to Jackson in 1966.

24. Floyd B. Barbour (ed.), *The Black Power Revolt* (Boston: Beacon, 1968), p. 65.

25. A particularly riveting example of this shift took place at the XIX Olympiad at Mexico City where Tommie Smith and John Carlos, the African American winners of the Gold and Bronze medals, lowered their heads and raised clenched fists in the Black Power salute during the playing of the Star-Spangled Banner. As Smith stated to the WABC-TV interviewer, Howard Cosell: "I wore a black right-hand glove and Carlos wore the left-hand glove of the same pair. My raised right hand stood for the power in black America. Carlos' raised left hand stood for the unity of black America. Together they formed an arch of unity and power. The black scarf around my neck stood for black pride. The black socks with no shoes stood for black poverty in America. The totality of our effort was the regaining of black dignity." From *A Hard Road to Glory— Track and Field: The African American Athlete in Track and Field* by Arthur Ashe, assisted by Kip Branch et al. (N.Y.: Amistad Press, 1988, reprinted 1993), p. 44.

26. Between 1966 and 1969, many "riots" took place in the United States from Newark, New Jersey and Washington, D.C. to Watts in Los Angeles, California. Most were in the North, Midwest and Western urban ghettos which, in many ways, simply exploded in frustration and rage. See the *Report of the National Advisory Commission on Civil Disorders* (New York: Bantam Books, 1968) which stated as its basic conclusion that "Our nation is moving toward two societies, one black, one white—separate and unequal." (p. 1).

27. Gayraud S. Wilmore and James H. Cone (eds.), *Black Theology: A Documentary History, 1966-1979* (Maryknoll, NY: Orbis, 1979), p. 44.

28. The most influential book by Malcolm X was published after his death, *The Autobiography of Malcolm X*, ed. Alex Haley (N.Y.: Grove Press, 1965); collections of his speeches include George Breitman, ed., *By Any Means Necessary* (N.Y.: Pathfinder Press, 1970), and *Malcolm X Speaks* (N.Y.: Grove Press, 1965); Archie Epps, ed., *The Speeches of Malcolm X at*

Harvard (William Morrow, 1968); *Malcolm X on Afro-American History* (Pathfinder Press, 1970); Bruce Perry, ed., *Malcolm X: The Last Speeches* (Pathfinder Press, 1989); also see his *Malcolm: The Life of a Man Who Changed Black America* (Barrytown, N.Y.: Station Hill, 1991); *Two Speeches by Malcolm X* (Merit Publishers, 1969), and David Gallen, ed., *A Malcolm X Reader: Perspectives on the Man and the Myths* (N.Y.: Carroll and Graf, 1994).

29. As stated in the *Directory of African American Religious Bodies* (compiled by the Howard University School of Divinity, Wardell J. Payne, ed.): "The American Muslim Mission (formerly known as the Nation of Islam) refers to itself as the 'lost nation of Islam.' It was founded by the Honorable Prophet Elijah Muhammad, who was born in Georgia as Elijah Poole (1897-1975). Poole changed his name to Elijah Muhammad as a sign of his conversion to Islam" (see pp. 136-143). He met W.D. Fard, a salesman, in Detroit and was instructed in Islam by him. After Fard's mysterious disappearance in 1934, Muhammad began to serve as the self-proclaimed messenger of Allah. His teachings were controversial and veered greatly from orthodox Islam, especially with regard to the "white" race which he saw as evil. After Muhammad's death, a schism occurred leading to the formation of the American Muslim Mission led by his son who renounced racial hatred and segregation and brought most of the members into alignment with orthodox Islam. A smaller group retained the name of the Nation of Islam under the leadership of Louis Farrakhan which retained the traditional stances of Elijah Muhammad.

30. See "The Ballot or the Bullet" speech in *Malcolm X Speaks*, pp. 23-44.

31. See especially the first and last chapters of this work.

32. "With Fanny Lou Hamer," in *Malcolm X Speaks*, p. 105.

33. In *A Testament of Hope*, p. 292.

34. James H. Cone, *Black Theology and Black Power*.

35. "Black Power Statement," in Cone and Wilmore, *Black Theology*, Vol. One, p. 23.

36. Ibid., p. 19.

37. See discussion in Chapter One.

38. See discussion in Chapters One and Two.

39. Joseph R. Washington, *Black Religion*, p. 143.

40. Ibid.

41. See "Black Theology and the Response of White Theologians," in Cone and Wilmore, eds., *Black Theology*, 1st ed. This section has not been included in the revised two volume edition published in 1993, as Wilmore noted that "...it does not seem so necessary to prove that Black Theology was both condemned and applauded by white scholars" in his "Introduction" to Volume One, p. 5.

42. Charles R. Lawrence, "The Separated Darker Brethren," *Christianity and Crisis* 25 (February 22, 1965), p. 18.

43. Washington's study was based on small Northern congregations rather than larger and more active congregations with trained ministers and actively involved and educated parishioners. Many critics saw this as severely limiting the value of the work.

44. Jerome H. Long, "Review of *Black Religion* by Joseph R. Washington," *Foundations* 7 (October 1964), p. 381.

45. James H. Cone, *For My People*, p. 9.

46. See Wilmore, *Black Religion and Black Radicalism*, esp. ch. 9.

47. If theology does not engage the issues arising "out of life in

society, especially the life of the oppressed," most Black (and other) liberation theologians would agree, it is neither Christian nor theology. See Evans, *We Have Been Believers*, especially Chapter 2, and Cone, *For My People*, pp. 28-29.

48. In later writings, Washington revised his more blatantly negative statements regarding Black religion and seemed more optimistic regarding the Black Church. See, for example, *The Politics of God* (Boston: Beacon Press, 1967).

49. See Albert Cleage, *The Black Messiah* (N.Y.: Sheed and Ward, 1968), and *Black Christian Nationalism: New Directions for the Black Church* (N.Y.: Morrow, 1972), founder of The Shrine of the Black Madonna. In the first work, he argues for the need for Blacks to develop, live, and worship independently of and apart from whites. He also asserts the actual literal blackness of Jesus Christ.

50. James H. Cone, *For My People*, p. 6.

4

The Sources and Norms of Black Liberation Theology

Black theology can be likened to a tree whose roots are African, whose trunk is Black with all of the richness and diversity of heritage that implies, and whose branches are the different forms that it takes within the United States as Protestant, Catholic and womanist and in South Africa and other lands of the African diaspora.[1] Therefore, in order to understand and, more importantly, do Black Theology, one must look at that tree from root to crown. As C. Eric Lincoln noted

> The Blacks brought their religion with them. After a time they accepted the white man's religion, but they have not always expressed it in the white man's way. It became the Blacks' purpose—perhaps destiny—to shape, to fashion, to re-create the religion offered them by the Christian slave master, to remold it nearer to their own heart's desire, nearer to their own peculiar needs. The Black religious experience is something more than a Black patina on a white happening. It is a unique response to a historical occurrence that can never be for any other people in America.[2]

James Cone cites the sources of Black Theology in his groundbreaking work, *A Black Theology of Liberation*, as the Black experience, Black history, Black culture, revelation, Scripture, and tradition, and the norm as Jesus Christ himself. These sources and norm remain valid to the present day.

> There is no truth for and about Black people that does not emerge out of the context of their experience. Truth in this sense is Black truth, a truth disclosed in the history and culture of Black people. This means that there can be no Black Theology which does not take the Black experience as a source for its starting point. Black Theology is a theology of and for Black people, an examination of their stories, tales, and sayings. It is an investigation of the mind into the raw materials of our pilgrimage, telling the story of "how we got over." For theology to be Black, it must reflect upon what it means to be Black. Black Theology must uncover the structures and forms of the Black experience, because the categories of interpretation must arise out of the thought forms of the Black experience itself.[3]

History, experience, and culture can be contained within the broader understanding of the Black historical experience. God is present and active in human experience. Human experience is the locus of God's involvement with all humanity, but most especially in the United States, with Black humanity who are and have been oppressed mainly because of their Blackness. God, therefore, serves as a validation for African Americans of their lives, their humanity, and their hoped-for, eventual freedom from all forms of oppression.

Gayraud Wilmore, even more than Cone originally, reflects on the importance of the Black experience, noting that "the first source of Black Theology is the Black community"[4] while the second source "may be found in the writings, sermons, and addresses of the Black preachers and public men and women of the past."[5] Wilmore calls for a Black hermeneutic (interpretation) which would "deal with the morphology of Black English, the meaning of Black music, poetry, the novel, the dance and...not only with the content, but the accent and cadence of blackness."[6] Lastly, he sees the traditional religions of Africa as a vital source for engaging in Black theology.[7]

> From the very beginning, Wilmore's concern was to create a black theology that was truly black—that is, African—and not a white version of Western Christianity colored black. He wanted the definition of black theology to be shaped by an African meaning of liberation and not simply by western bourgeois ideas of freedom and equality, as a Marxist idea of liberation.[8]

The emphasis, then, in Black Theology was on an understanding of liberation as shaped and formed by the Black historical experience. Two meanings, in particular, emerged:

> One emphasized socio-political freedom as derived from the biblical theme of the Exodus and nineteenth century Black freedom fighters. The other emphasized cultural liberation as derived from the black nationalism of Henry McNeale Turner, Marcus Garvey, Malcolm X, and especially the religions of Africa.[9]

Revelation and Scripture are equally important for Black Theology. For it is the revelation of God's action in the world as revealed to Black Americans that has enabled them to withstand the rigors of their life. This revelation occurred, and continues to occur, not in miraculous acts which "break into" and disrupt history but in the many seemingly uneventful acts which have enabled the slaves and their descendants to make it "one day at a time." The Word of God broke open the truth to them of God's love for them and all who are oppressed. It served as the source for their first theologizing in the spirituals for the Scriptures, especially the Old Testament, and gave them the words and the vision to proclaim their faith, a faith radically at odds with that imposed upon them by their masters.

Today Black biblical scholars, such as Cain Felder, Randall Bailey and others,[10] are building upon the foundational work laid by Charles Copher who can be called the father of modern critical Black Biblical hermeneutics.[11] They are revealing the active and central presence, so long ignored or denied, of Blacks in Sacred Scripture and developing new interpretations that make connections with Black and African history and experience.

Black Americans first clearly experienced God in the dehumanizing experience of slavery in the United States. It was in that experience that the kernel of truth relating to Black being was first revealed to Blacks themselves. For years they were taught that God was a God who favored the slave masters, one who taught that the slaves' only duty was to be obedient and to serve their master well. But as they learned to read the Bible for themselves, they realized the lie being taught them. They read of a God of freedom, one whose total identity and activity was with the poor and powerless rather than the wealthy and powerful, as prophesied by Amos, Hosea and Micah. They read of a God who set a people, an enslaved people like themselves, free and carried them to a new land where he became their God and they became his people (the Exodus). And they read of a God who so loved the poor and the oppressed that he became one with them, a human being born into the world of the poor, condemned to death and dying for their freedom (the Gospels, especially Luke). They read and they believed.[12]

But they were not an educated people; they were a people of the fields and kitchens with no more than rudimentary learning and basic beliefs. Thus, their experience of this liberating God and his compassionate love for them was more than they could fully comprehend initially. Their inarticulateness gave rise to feelings of joy, feelings of comfort in times of sorrow, feelings of help in times of need. They recognized, in this experience, that they were being addressed by an Other and they rejoiced even while not fully understanding. They had a theology without knowing it.

They expressed their experience of God in song, story, and prayer, while continuing to look for that day of redemption when they would be freed from the shackles of slavery. It was in these songs, stories, and prayers that they kept alive their hope and faith and, in return, were given the strength to "keep on keeping on."[13]

Tradition, the final source for Black Theology, is both that of Christianity from its earliest beginnings in the Middle East and Africa to the present day and also the critical reflection of Black Americans upon that tradition from their own particular faith perspective. Thus it calls upon them to know and to understand that tradition in order to be able to faithfully critique its distortion during the period of slavery in this country and to the present day, in both Black and white churches. It requires them to go even further, however, "back to Africa" to retrieve the legacy of their African forefathers and foremothers whose interaction with God has withstood centuries. In order to articulate a theology which speaks truly of their own long-lived relationship with God, they realized they must first learn their own history and the language of that history.

For Black Christians, the only norm for their theologizing is Jesus Christ. It is through the lens of Christ's salvific life, death and resurrection that they are able to reconcile the harshness of their lives and the hope that dwells within them. For James Evans, as well as other Black theologians, "The norm both authorizes and legitimates theological discourse...." This norm is grounded in "the notion that the acme of God's self-revelation is the identity and mission of the person and work of Jesus Christ...."[14] This can be seen as

> two aspects of a single reality: the liberation of Blacks and the revelation of Jesus Christ.... The norm of all God-talk which seeks to be black-talk is the manifestation of Jesus as the black Christ who provides the necessary soul for black liberation.[15]

It is through this lens, that of the Black historical experience (encompassing Black experience, history, and culture) in the United States and the role that Christianity and Jesus Christ have played in that experience, that we can begin our discussion of the Black theologians who have emerged over the past twenty-five years since the publication of the Black Power Manifesto.

Black Theologians: Political and Cultural

Dwight Hopkins outlines, in *Black Theology: USA and South Africa*,[16] two perspectives on Black Theology, one cultural, the other political. This division is helpful in providing an overview of the major contributors to Black Theology in its first two stages and their varying approaches and methodologies, thus revealing the rich diversity present within the field itself. However, it is not as useful in categorizing the emerging second generation of Black scholars in theology, both male and female, who, having perhaps learned from the mistakes and omissions of their predecessors, are less easy to put in one or the other camp. Instead, as do the earlier scholars who are still writing, they have tended to merge the political and the cultural under the umbrella of the Black experience in the United States. In addition, they, like Cone, Wilmore, Roberts, and others, are more open to input and critique from other liberation theologies developing both within the United States (such as Hispanic American, feminist, Asian American and others) and outside of the USA (Latin America, South Africa, South Korea, Asia, the Caribbean, etc.) and, in turn, serve to provide a necessary critique of these theologies.

The political theologians are depicted as seeing theology as a mandate for political activism on the part of the Black Church and community and for the full empowerment of Blacks, while the cultural theologians, while not totally disagreeing with this emphasis, assert that, prior to political action, one must first be in touch with the cultural context from which that call to action arises. Hopkins sees James Cone, Major Jones, Albert Cleage and J. Deotis Roberts as representative of the political group,[17] while Gayraud Wilmore, Charles Long, Cecil Cone and Vincent Harding are members of the cultural.[18]

James Cone's assertion that the only true Christian theology is one expressed in terms of God acting in history on the side of the poor and oppressed clearly presents a combined theological and political message. For him, such an understanding is an active option which overrides all other theological understandings.

I believe that Christian theology achieves its distinctive identity when it takes on the issues of those who are struggling to be human in an oppressive world. Christians believe that their faith has something to say about this world and about the human beings in it— something that can make a distinctive difference in the quality of life. It is therefore the task of theology to demonstrate the difference that the gospel can and does make in human lives, using the resources of the scriptures and traditions of the churches as well as other modern tools of social, historical, cultural, economic and philosophical analysis.[19]

Black Theology is, therefore, necessarily a theology of, by and for Black peoples while God/Christ are Black because the victims with whom they are in solidarity are oppressed simply because of their blackness. This blackness is seen in different ways—ontologically (Cone), symbolically (Roberts) or physically (Cleage)—but the critical point being made is that the Blackness of God/Christ reveals God/Christ's oneness with Black people in their oppression as a positive option on God's part.

The theologians of culture, on the other hand, while agreeing on the importance of placing God/Christ on the side of the oppressed in their struggle for liberation, note that in order to fully understand and express that theology, there must first be a return to and retrieval of the roots of the Black experience, especially African Americans' cultural ties with Africa as well as the experiences which have shaped and formed them into a new people in their new homeland. One must, thus, look at the history, music, literature, art, etc. of Black people in order to develop the foundation upon which a true Black Theology can emerge. For without a past, a future cannot be dreamed of. Thus, in one sense, the cultural theologians would appear to be more open to the input of non-Christian as well as non-religious sources in their understanding and development of a viable Black Theology. However, it can still be stated that all Black theologians see Black Theology as a theology of praxis emerging from the breadth and depth of the Black experience which, while recognizing the promise of the eschaton as revealed in Christ, also demands concrete action in this world on behalf of marginalized Blacks in American society today.

As the new generation of theologians present their perspective, we see that the boundaries of these categories, political and cultural, tend now to merge and overlap rather than being distinct, if ever they truly were. As some voices drop out and others make their contributions, Black Theology continues to grow and develop, taking on new challenges in the political realm while refining its thought in those areas customarily recognized as part of the theological debate, as will be seen in the following chapters.

Notes

1. The Black Theology of the United States has influenced and been influenced by the Black Theology of South Africa; see Dwight Hopkins, *Black Theology: US and South Africa*. Also see Itumeleng Mosala, *The Unquestionable Right To Be Free: Black Theology from South Africa* (Maryknoll, N.Y.: Orbis Books, 1986), who incorporates the work of many South African Black theologians as well as works on African Theology and U.S. Black Theology such as Josiah Young, *Black Theology and African Theology: Siblings or Distant Cousins?* (Maryknoll, N.Y.: Orbis Books, 1986), on African Theology such as Emmanuel Martey, *African Theology: Inculturation and Liberation* (Maryknoll: Orbis, 1993) and on Caribbean Theology.

2. Foreword to the First Edition, Wilmore, *Black Religion*, p. vii.

3. James H. Cone, *God of the Oppressed* (New York: Seabury, 1975), p. 18.

4. *Black Religion*, 2nd ed., p. 235.

5. Ibid., p. 236.

6. Ibid., p. 237.

7. Ibid., Chapter 1.

8. Cone, *For My People*, p. 61.

9. Ibid., p. 62.

10. See Cain Felder, *Troubling Biblical Waters: Race, Class and Family* (Maryknoll, N.Y.: Orbis, 1989); Felder, ed., *Stony The Road We Trod: African American Biblical Interpretation* (Minneapolis: Fortress Press, 1991); Renita Weems, *Just a Sister Away: A Womanist Vision of Women's Relationships in the Bible* (San Diego: LuraMedia, 1988); Randall Bailey and Jacqueline Grant, eds., *The Recovery of Black Presence: An Interdisciplinary Exploration* (Nashville: Abingdon Press, 1995); and others including David Shannon, Thomas Hoyt, Jr., Clarice Martin, and Vincent Wimbush.

11. The long-awaited first anthology of Dr. Copher's work has been published as *Black Biblical Studies: An Anthology of Charles B. Copher: Biblical and Theological Issues on the Black Presence in the Bible* (Chicago: Black Light Fellowship, 1993).

12. So much so that most of the early slave rebellions were led by Black slaves who were allowed to preach and exhort their fellow slaves and saw themselves as being on a mission from God to set their people free. The result of these revolts was the imposition of the harsh Black Codes, forerunners of post-bellum "Jim Crow" laws, which made teaching a slave to read illegal and possession of the Bible a crime.

13. See Cone, *The Spirituals and the Blues,* Hopkins and Cummings, *Cut Loose Your Stammering Tongue,* Hopkins, *Shoes That Fit Our Feet* and Evans, *We Have Been Believers.* This sense of God's active presence in their lives now rather than only as a promise for the future is very much in keeping with the West African understanding of time where the future is not far off but everpresent, see Wood, p. 173: "The Christian's belief that one's earthly life should be spent preparing for an ultimate place called heaven was based on a concept—the future, or perhaps...eternity—that the African found difficult to understand.... While white Christians envisioned spending eternity in heaven, black converts were inclined to anticipate a more worldly 'Day of Judgement.' ...(T)he slave focused on a definite point in the future when he would be relieved of his burdens, not on a vague infinity in which everyone would simply be happy."

14. However, this norm is seen in critically different ways. Womanist theologian Delores Williams critiques, for example, what she sees as a Black male bias and reinterprets the norm of Jesus Christ from a womanist perspective, one which debates the present-day value of surrogate suffering, on the part of Jesus, and as historically lived out by Black women. Other womanist theologians, Kelly Brown Douglas and Jacquelyn Grant, among others, also present a radically different perspective of Jesus Christ which will be discussed in greater detail in Chapter Eight of this work.

15. Cone, *A Black Theology of Liberation,* p. 38; see also his *God of the Oppressed,* which more fully explores the Black understanding of God incarnate in Jesus Christ.

16. (Maryknoll, N.Y.: Orbis, 1989).

17. See Hopkins, *Black Theology,* Chapter 1. The writings of Cleage and Cone have already been cited above. Major Jones is the author of *Black Awareness: A Theology of Hope* (Nashville: Abingdon Press, 1971), *Black Christian Ethics* (Nashville: Abingdon Press, 1974), and *The Color of God: The Concept of*

God in Afro-American Thought (Macon, GA.: Mercer University Press, 1987), and J. Deotis Roberts has authored *Liberation and Reconciliation: A Black Theology* (Philadelphia: Westminster Press, 1971; republished Orbis Books, 1994), *A Black Political Theology* (Philadelphia: Westminster Press, 1974), *Black Theology Today* (N.Y.: Edwin Mellen Press, 1983), and *Black Theology in Dialogue* (Philadelphia: Westminster Press, 1987).

18. See Ibid., chapter 2. Besides his seminal work, *Black Religion* and the two volume documentary history co-edited with Cone, Wilmore has authored *Black and Presbyterian: The Heritage and the Hope* (Philadelphia: Geneva Press, 1983) and *Last Things First* (Philadelphia: Westminster Press, 1982) and is editor of *African American Religious Studies* (Durham, N.C.: Duke University Press, 1989). Charles Long is the author of *Significations: Signs, Symbols, and Images in the Interpretation of Religion* (Philadelphia: Fortress Press, 1986), while Cecil Cone wrote *The Identity Crisis in Black Theology* (Nashville: The African Methodist Episcopal Church, 1975). Vincent Harding is the author of several works including *There Is a River: The Black Struggle for Freedom in America* (New York: Harcourt Brace Jovanovich, 1981), *The Other American Revolution* (Los Angeles: Center for Afro-American Studies and Atlanta: Institute of the Black World, 1980), and *Hope and History* (Maryknoll, N.Y.: Orbis Books, 1990).

19. Cone, *For My People*, pp. 28-29.

5

Symbol and Metaphor in Black Liberation Theology

As can be seen in the preceding chapters, those who do Black Theology have developed that theology in similar yet strikingly different ways. For all, the context of Black Americans is the foundation for their theologizing, but the methodologies used and emphases differ, resulting in overlapping yet critically nuanced theological voices.

This and the following chapter will explore the different forms that Black Theology has taken since its development. In this chapter, we will address the use of symbol and metaphor in the work of various Black theologians in presenting the Christian message in a form that is representative of and also comprehensible to Black Americans. Chapter Six will further develop the understanding of narrative and testimony which informs the work of Black theologians.

For all, the starting point is the human situation, human experience, but, to reiterate, the central focus of Black Theology is a particular human experience, that of peoples of African descent in the United States. Their anthropology centers on Black humanity, around whom their theological investigations are organized. Thus, doctrine, spirituality and discipline are systematized with respect to the interpretation which arises from the Black perspective.[1] Any experience, to be genuinely and authentically Christian, must be identified as such by the Christian community and, for Black Theology, that community is Black.

Christ is the "Black" Christ, Black because he has identified himself in his Incarnation with the poor and the oppressed.[2] He is, as seen in Chapter Four, the norm by which the interpretation given by the Black historical experience is structured, presented and validated. But it is that experience which also interprets the meaning of Christ as God's revelation today. For God is always present in human experience.

Theology emerges from a people's efforts to understand themselves in relation to God. Yet God is always and everywhere incomprehensible mystery. As St. Augustine realized, if we have understood, then what we have understood is not God. In our finite human efforts to understand God then, it is necessary to draw on symbols and other means that are couched in human terms, in human understandings, while recognizing their inability to fully reveal the totality of God. We look at ourselves as created in the image of God in an effort to see and understand who God is to and for us. Human experience is the locus of God's involvement with humanity and, thus, is the beginning of theological reflection.

Themes

Symbol, metaphor, narrative and testimony are obviously correlated. They can be exemplified in terms of the doctrine of God/Christ (both symbol and metaphor), the

Black story/history (narrative), and the witness of the
Black community and the Black Church (testimony). For
the symbol of a Creator God and Christ who liberate, the
metaphor of God and Christ as Black, the narrative of
the history of Black people in the United States and the
testimony of their lives, is the foundation for any and all
Black religious discourse. It helps one to understand the
hope-filled belief of African Americans in their eventual
freedom, one social, economic, and physical as well as
eschatological, and their conviction that such freedom
can and ultimately will come from God alone.

A Black Hermeneutic

In studying the nature of language and symbol, we
realize that

> ...man can only understand his own existence, can only
> understand himself, through the signs—personal and
> cultural—scattered in the world, and he only under-
> stands as he interprets those signs.[3]

Interpretation, the discernment of a hidden meaning
in an apparent sense, is vital. It is only in the building of
meaning that a person becomes who he or she is, and
that meaning can only be built up through interpretation of the signs of the world.

Black scholars, thus, have sought to develop a new
hermeneutic, one which is in alignment with their consciousness of themselves as a people of faith and struggle.
Henry Mitchell, recognizing this need, notes:

> Just as the new hermeneutic of Ebeling and others has
> sought to recapture the vital message of Luther and the
> Reformation Fathers for the benefit of their sons, so must
> the Black hermeneutic seek to look into the message of

the Black past and see what the Black Fathers could be saying to Black people today.[4]

Gayraud Wilmore takes a similar stance:

[A Black hermeneutic] has to do with the intricate work of unpacking the mythology, folklore, and ethical norms of the black community as reflected in its oral tradition and literature, in order to uncover the ways in which blacks have linguistically and otherwise communicated their provisional and ultimate concerns and solutions in an exploitative and racist society....[5]

Thus, for Wilmore, such a Black hermeneutic must encompass "the morphology of black English, the meaning of black music, poetry, the novel, the dance" while also incorporating, as Mitchell has suggested, not only the content, but the accent and cadence of Black preaching.[6]

Symbol in Black Theology

Symbols are those signs which develop, change, or grow in meaning, as they move from one world-view to another. As world-views change and develop, so are symbols enriched or impoverished of meaning, for the one influences the other and vice versa.

Thus, a symbol or set of symbols cannot have meaning independently of a particular encompassing world-view. For Christians, regardless of race, ethnicity or denomination, this controlling symbol, historically, has been Jesus Christ as the sign of the unique revelation of God. It is this symbol which establishes the foundation of and provides the criterion for being Christian; for to be a Christian, regardless of denomination, means to believe in and be a follower of Jesus the Christ.

The Black Christian understanding of Christ is not, however, nor can it be, identical to that of others due to the particular exigencies of Black life in the United States. Black humanity in the United States has always understood itself in terms of those understandings of Jesus which arose, as shown, from the experience of slavery and oppression. Black American men and women, therefore, understand themselves by relating to those signs which emerged from their constant struggle for freedom, from the songs, stories, and witness of individual Blacks and the Black community as a whole. These signs define who they are in the world, over against a world-view which has relied, too often, on negative depictions of Black humanity as the basis for symbolizing blackness. It is these negative images which African Americans seek to destroy, replacing them with a perspective of Black people which recognizes and upholds their human dignity and worth. The language of struggle, resistance, and defiance, as well as that of pride, affirmation and self-determination has emerged from the Black community itself and thus serves as valid defining images of that community.

It is this language, of a people who demand respect and equality for themselves, which gave birth anew to the liberating symbols of a God who created all of humanity in God's own image and sent God's Son, the warrior Christ, to bring about that liberation, which were raised up during the Civil Rights Movement of the 1960s to confound and subvert the prevailing negative world-view. Blackness, therefore, became beautiful, a sign of blessing rather than a curse.

God and Christ as Symbolic of Black Liberation

The preeminent symbol or redeeming sign for the empowerment and affirmation of African Americans is the God/Christ[7] of the liberation struggle, the "Black" Christ who is the unique revelation of a "Black" God. God, as Creator, and Christ, as Liberator, are the symbols which provide the hermeneutical principle for Black Theology, one "which is in harmony with the Black condition and the biblical revelation,"[8] which pays attention to the encounter of the Black community with God's emancipative liberation and which springs forth from that encounter. It is this which validates theologizing from the Black perspective.

Christ, the sign of God's expression of solidarity with, especially, Black humanity, was first experienced in slavery as the slaves resisted the imposition of a Christianity which upheld both their debasement and their enslavement. An illiterate people for the most part, they were yet able to envision a God whose total identity and activity was with them as God had been centuries before with the enslaved Hebrews. This encounter with a God both stern and loving inspired them to express their theological understanding in ways that were in keeping with their theological naiveté. They spoke of being "struck dead" or "struck wide open" by their encounter with God in their conversion experiences.[9] For them, the "essential being of Jesus is freedom" and that understanding provided them with a means of understanding and fighting against their own situation with its "man-made" rather than God-ordained constraints.[10]

Their expression poured forth in song, the spirituals which told of a land where all would be free one day; in story, the tales of Br'er Rabbit and High John the Conqueror, symbols of the weak winning over the strong, not by revolution or strength, but by cunning and outwitting the boss; and in prayer, the prayers of a troubled people trying to "make it over" while searching for a life of decency and humanity on this earth.[11]

This slave theology served African Americans ably for several centuries and to a certain extent is still present today, serving as a foundation for the more systematically articulated Black Theology that emerged in the 1960s. It was this expression of the experience of God and his Incarnate Son, and what it meant to them, their interpretation of the signs of God working in their very midst maintaining and sustaining them, which enabled African Americans to survive and struggle onward. It is especially in the spirituals that the symbol of God/Christ as liberator is most fully encountered. As James Cone realized,

> It is the spirituals that show us the essence of black religion, that is the experience of trying to be free in the midst of a "powerful lot of tribulation."
>
>> Oh Freedom! Oh Freedom!
>> Oh Freedom, I love thee!
>> And before I'll be a slave,
>> I'll be buried in my grave,
>> And go home to my Lord and be free.
>
> The spirituals are songs about black souls, "stretching out into the outskirts of God's eternity" and affirming the Word that makes you know that you are a human being—no matter what white people say. Throughout the song, black people were able to affirm that Spirit who was continuous with their existence as free beings; and they created a new style of religious worship. They shouted and they prayed; they preached and they sang, because *they had found something.* They encountered a new reality; a new God not enshrined in white churches and religious gatherings.[12]

Dwight Hopkins also captures this "other" way of understanding God's action in Black lives:

In the "Invisible Institution," the slaves displayed a remarkable clarity concerning the cultural dimension of their theology. They knew that God spoke to them in their own medium. In fact, African American chattel could not worship God truthfully unless they "talked" with God through their black culture.[13]

God was a warrior God whose intervention led to their freedom as a result of the Civil War; God was a just God who did not abide the sins of their masters for long; God was a saving and liberating God whose promise of salvation was both personal (spiritual) and communitarian (physical) for all who believed and maintained their faith, but God was also a loving mother who nurtured and sustained her children in their struggle.[14]

But as slavery gave way to a freedom that too often, especially in the South, proved in its own way to be merely symbolic, the experience of God/Christ as Liberator was severely challenged. This was partly due to the failure of that same Black Church which, founded as a sign of freedom and independence, had been co-opted into the status-quo mentality of the white dominant society of the United States that continued to preach their inherent inferiority and a passive faith with its rewards coming only in the hereafter. However, it was also due to the constant and overwhelming odds against them, their growing frustration at "too little too late" and the increasing threat to the sustaining force of the Black community brought about by migration, dispersal, and a constant, grating poverty. Yet the songs, the stories, and the prayers were still there and they were still being listened to.

Although the Black Church and its theology seemed to lie dormant during the early part of the twentieth century, Blacks were still engaged in on-going reflection on their experience. It was this reflection which was the foundation for the courageous and often self-sacrificing acts of those who participated in the Civil Rights and Black Power Movements of the 1960s. That reflection was not on a new symbol but on the same symbol reclaimed, reaffirmed, and renewed.

Blacks began to reflect, as their slave forebears had, on the meaning and significance of God/Christ for them in their present situation in the latter half of the twentieth century and on the meaning of their existence in the United States as a still oppressed and marginalized people. They began to raise challenging questions concerning the existence and reality of that same God/Christ which only they themselves could answer: Who is God for us? How can we worship a God who apparently does not recognize the legitimacy of Black humanity? These questions burned to the very core of Black existence. For, like their ancestors, they recognized God, especially in God's incarnation as Jesus, as the answer to which their often pain-filled and desperate existence was the powerfully poignant question.

As Christians, they turned once again to Scripture to re-examine *for themselves* who this God was, what he meant to them, and what was the meaning of their present suffering. There, they became reacquainted with a God in solidarity with the poor, one who showed partiality to the oppressed by sending God's only Son "to preach good news to the poor, to proclaim release to captives and recovery of sight to the blind, to set at liberty those who are oppressed" (Lk 4:18). Twentieth century African Americans, in company with their forebears, realized that

Jesus' death on the cross represented God's boundless solidarity with victims, even unto death. Jesus' resurrection is the good news that there is new life for the poor that is not determined by their poverty but overcomes it; and this new life is available to all. Jesus' resurrection is God's victory over oppression. If this biblical message has any meaning for contemporary America, it must mean that black power represents God's resurrection in Jesus becoming embodied in the consciousness and actions of black America.[15]

Meaning was, thus, restored to their lives, the meaning of God as one who was on their side. It meant, therefore, that they, as a people, also had meaning, a meaning bound up in that of God's. They, like the children of Israel, were the Chosen Ones of God. But to be the new Israelites, they had to believe.

Belief requires commitment. It requires a faith that must be professed, despite the fact that all questions have not yet been answered and the way is still a rough and rocky one. It is the experience of God as Liberator which leads to the acceptance of God in one's own being as constitutive of one's own nature.

Having progressed from experiencing the symbol of God and having wagered their very lives on the truth of their paradoxical interpretation of that symbol, Black Christians then recovered this liberating symbol by re-experiencing it, this time in the fullness of its meaning, a fullness enriched by ongoing reflection, by ongoing critique, and, most importantly, by ongoing faith.

It is in this experiencing of God/Christ the Liberator as a second naiveté, one which has overcome the immediacy, the uncritical and unknowing nature of that first inarticulate experience, or naiveté, that Black Theology arises. Black Theology is an attempt to give meaning, in the form of written language, to that symbol of God/Christ which the Black community has experienced over the four hundred-plus years since their arrival on these shores. It is an attempt to name God/Christ in Black language, one stemming from and inclusive of their self-understanding and self-affirmation as confirmed by that same God/Christ.

This is no different from what has been done throughout human history seen as the effort of humanity to understand both itself and God.

Karl Rahner perceived that "the personal history of the experience of the self is the personal history of the experience of God...the personal history of the experience of God signifies, over and above itself, the personal history of the experience of the self."[16]

Building upon this, Elizabeth Johnson notes:

> ...the experience of God which is never directly available is mediated...through the changing history of oneself.... Personal development of the self also constitutes development of the experience of God; loss of self-identity is also the loss of the experience of God.[17]

With this understanding, it is relevant that Cone approaches the question of God for Blacks in terms, initially, of God-language, asserting that God's reality is presupposed but that it is up to the theologian to analyze the nature of that reality in terms of its meaning to and for the community that is living that reality. He raises a critical question: Is God merely a symbolic word which, if it loses its power to point to the meaning of Black life, must therefore be destroyed? In order to have an authentic faith, the oppressed, he argues, may have to renounce their faith in a God who has been used by the oppressor solely to oppress. The question, therefore, is not whether Blacks believe in God but in whose God? After raising the question, Cone concludes, however, that God-language must be retained in Black Theology because it is the source of the Black community's identification with the divine presence. In order for Black Theology to remain Black and in touch with the Black community, which is its source, it must, therefore, use those symbols arising from that community rather than develop new and alien ones.[18]

However, this does not mean acquiescing in the biased interpretation of God or Christ that has been disseminated by the dominant society in America. It is necessary to disclose the "white" God as a false God, an idol who must be destroyed, while yet retaining faith in God, the true Black God, of liberation. For Cone, this means, therefore, that God-talk cannot be Christian talk unless it is related directly to the liberation of the oppressed. It is necessary that the oppressed themselves define the structure and scope of that reality.[19]

The Black struggle, for Cone, is a manifestation of God as God. God is using that struggle to show God's people that their lives do have meaning and that Christ, in his Incarnation, enters human affairs and takes the side of the oppressed. The Gospel is a Gospel of liberation. It is the source of Black belief in God's nature as being that of one on the side of the poor. It is the historical Christ of the Gospel who confirms that divine solidarity not only by his birth in poverty but also by his life's ministry, which is an unequivocal proclamation of solidarity with the victims, and, finally and most importantly, by his ignominious death and his glorious resurrection. Jesus died the death of a common criminal who, at the end, has lost all but his faith in his Father. He was resurrected as the Savior, victorious over death and all forms of sin.

For Black Theology, God is present in all dimensions of human liberation. Jesus' life and death are the revelation of the freedom of God, who takes upon himself the totality of human oppression. His resurrection discloses God's victory over oppression and its transformation into the possibility of human freedom.

Other Black theologians, apart from William Jones,[20] affirm this Black understanding of God as one who intervenes on the side of the oppressed, a God who differs significantly from the God preached to Blacks and others in their marginalized situation. It is this understanding which is at the heart of the slave narratives as noted earlier.

This same God is also the One who gave freely of the divine self in the Incarnation as Jesus of Nazareth. This man Jesus is the symbol to Black Christians of all that is hopeful and promised of a better world not only after death but of its possibility here on this earth:

> He is the Word in their lives, and thus to speak of their experience as it is manifested in the joys and sorrows of black life is to speak of the One they say is the 'Comforter in the time of trouble,' 'the Lily of the Valley,' and 'the bright morning star.'[21]

Jesus Christ and the Black experience converge in the Incarnation because God became man in Jesus Christ. He disclosed the divine will to be with humanity in its wretchedness:

> And because we blacks accept his presence in Jesus as the true definition of our humanity, blackness and divinity are dialectically bound together as one reality. This is the theological meaning of the paradoxical assertion about the primacy of the black experience and Jesus Christ as witnessed in Scripture.[22]

God and Jesus Christ as Metaphor

As God/Christ are the symbols, par excellence, for African Americans of their humanity and their liberation, so the understanding of God/Christ as Black serves as an empowering metaphor which challenges and, ultimately, shifts reality.

It is in the metaphorical depiction of God/Christ in Black Theology that the widest variation in the understanding of, especially, the earliest Black theologians can be found. The statement that "God and Christ are Black"[23] takes on different meanings depending on the theological stance of the theologian presenting it.

A metaphor is, in many ways, a logical absurdity, involving a twist or shift of meaning from one level of understanding to another. It can be seen as a calculated error, not in the sense of being incorrect, but in that it brings together understandings which are apparently opposite or contradictory to each other.

> ...precisely by means of this calculated error metaphor discloses a relationship of meaning hitherto unnoticed between terms which were prevented from communicating by former classifications.[24]

To call this statement regarding God/Christ a calculated error is not, thus, to imply that it is erroneous but to call attention to what *appears* to be erroneous because of its act of bringing together two understandings thought to be totally incompatible, the being of God/Christ with the being of Black humanity, thereby totally startling the reader/observer/listener into a new and paradoxical awareness.

By calling God/Christ Black, James Cone is expressing a *true* metaphor. It is true because it is a metaphor "in which a new extension of the meaning of the words answers a novel discordance in the sentence."[25] New meaning is created, one which expands our language and creates a new reality, a necessary aspect of doing theology. As it is the function of language to articulate our experience of the world and to give form to that experience, this is exactly what Cone and other Black theologians are doing. They are articulating the experience of the Black community's encounter with God as the One who has and continues to set them free. Christ and God are therefore Black because those who are oppressed in the United States and who call upon God/Christ to relieve their oppression are themselves Black:

> Since the black community is an oppressed community because, and only because, of its blackness, the Christological importance of Jesus Christ must be found in his blackness. If he is not black as we are, then the resurrection has little significance for our times. Indeed, if he cannot be what we are, we cannot be who he is. Our being with him is dependent on his being with us in the oppressed black condition, revealing to us what is necessary for our liberation.[26]

This understanding is just as important for marginalized Black Christians today as the assertion of Jesus' conjoined humanity and divinity was for the early Church.

Cone is not asserting, however, that Christ, in his actual physical being, is or ever was a physically Black man in skin color. Blackness must be seen, in Cone's view, as "a manifestation of the being of God in that it reveals that neither divinity nor humanity resides in white definitions but in the liberation from black captivity."[27]

The literal color of Jesus is, finally, irrelevant to Cone. Although in his theology he is referring to a specific community of people who are Black not only in skin-color but also in thought, word, and commitment, he does not see "blackness" as a restrictive term, as one limited to a certain race of people. Rather, to be Black encompasses, to him, all who are oppressed whether for reasons of gender, race, or class, or all who take sides with the oppressed by joining, with body as well as mind, in the front lines of their struggle for liberation.

The Black community is, therefore, a means for understanding that God's acts in history are acts of liberation on behalf of those oppressed, and that Christ's life, death and resurrection are the signs of God's having chosen them as his people.

> In a revolutionary situation, there can never be just theology. It is always theology identified with a particular community. It is either identified with those who oppress or with its victims.[28]

Thus, in his attempt to describe God and his revelatory activity, Cone can be said to draw upon the Tillichian notion that humanity cannot describe God directly but must do so through symbols which point to dimensions of reality that cannot be spoken of literally.[29]

> Symbols point beyond themselves to something else, something moreover in which they participate. They open up levels of reality which otherwise are closed for us, and concomitantly open up depths of our own being, which otherwise would remain untouched. They cannot be produced intentionally but from a deep level that Tillich identifies as the collective unconscious. Finally, they grow and die like living beings in relation to their power to bear the presence of the divine in changing cultural situations.[30]

To speak in terms of blackness, therefore, is to speak both symbolically and metaphorically, in terms of a reality which is omnipresent in this country, that of the oppressed situation of Black Americans and the impact this has had and continues to have on them with regard to their language about self and God:

The focus on blackness does not mean that only blacks suffer as victims in a racist society, but that blackness is an ontological symbol of a visible reality which best describes what oppression means in America....Blackness, then, stands for all victims of oppression who realize that their humanity is inseparable from man's liberation from whiteness.[31]

It is by means of the "shocking" statement that "God/Christ is Black" that attention is called, not only to the plight of the oppressed, but also to that of the oppressor. Cone's provocative statement demands a new look at the reality of Black and white existence in the United States. It is because the statement "God/Christ is Black" comes as such a shock that he is able through his theology to reveal the continued presence of racism, racial prejudice and discrimination in America. No one is shocked to hear that God/Christ may be white; that has been the prevailing assumption, despite the fact that he was born a Jew in the Middle East. It is in just that juxtaposition of one reality with another which is totally, in the opinion of many, not only unrelated but actually almost heretical that the metaphor is born and that it works and a "new vision of reality springs up."[32]

Thus, Cone, in his reality-shattering statement, creates a "memorable" metaphor, one which "has the power of cognitively and effectively relating two separate domains by using language appropriate to the one as a lens for seeing the other."[33] He says a reality that could not have been said in the normal terms of discourse and, thereby, succeeds in changing reality.

Contrary to Cone, Albert Cleage, founder of the Shrine of the Black Madonna and leader of the Black Christian Nationalism Movement, asserts that "Jesus was a black revolutionary Zealot, leading the fight against a white

Rome in order to realize a revolution for the black nation of Israel."[34]

> When I say that Jesus was black, that Jesus was the black Messiah...I'm not saying, "Wouldn't it be nice if Jesus was black?" or "Let's pretend that Jesus was black" or "It's necessary psychologically for us to believe that Jesus was black." I'm saying that Jesus WAS black. There never was a white Jesus.[35]

Cleage's understanding of Jesus is grounded in his vision of him as a political revolutionary whose sole purpose is to institute the Black nation. He is more concerned with the Jesus of history whose Gospel is one of liberation rather than the resurrected Christ who symbolizes in his view an "other-worldly" salvation.[36] Thus, his emphasis is on Black nationalism which has led to his emphasis on Black separation from the white world and the development of his independent church.

Jesus, for J. Deotis Roberts whose theology places an emphasis on reconciliation, is

> the black Messiah [who] speaks to a psychocultural crisis engendered by white American religion's demand that only the white Christ is worthy of adoration.... A need materializes to make Christ and the gospel address the black person directly. As a black image Christ becomes one among black people, and the black person retrieves his or her own dignity and pride.[37]

In affirming a Black Christ, Roberts makes room for a white Christ as well, arguing that forcing white Americans to worship a Black Christ would be equally as dehumanizing for them as worshiping a white Christ has been for Blacks. However, in his efforts to balance liberation and reconciliation as the twin poles of his methodology, he believes that if whites could come to acknowledge a Black Christ, reconciliation between Blacks and whites would become more viable. Yet, in the final analysis, he sees true reconciliation as going beyond color to the acceptance of a "universal Christ" who is colorless.[38] As Hopkins notes, for Roberts:

> The black Messiah functions in a symbolic and mythic capacity. In the black experience the black Messiah liberates blacks. At the same time the universal Christ reconciles black and white Americans. Jesus Christ the Liberator offers liberation from white oppression and forgiveness from sin and exploitation within the black community. Jesus Christ the Reconciler brings black people together and black and white people together in "multi-racial fellowship."[39]

To be Black in the United States is to be oppressed, to be discriminated against, solely and specifically, because of one's color and what that color signifies to the oppressor. To view reality from an oppressed perspective, one must become "Black," not necessarily physically but ontologically. One must adopt the situation of the oppressed in America and live in it and work to overcome it. The theologians discussed would all agree that no one can speak on behalf of another's plight without sharing in the experience of that person or that person's community. To attempt to do so is to place oneself above others as one who decides invalidly on the validity of their claims and their expressions. Thus, white theologians, because of their initial failure and refusal to participate in what it means to be Black in America, are judged incapable of speaking about the meaning of God and the Gospel of Jesus Christ to those who continue to be oppressed because of their blackness. They cannot be allowed to do so, for the language is not the same nor can the interpretation of that language be the same.[40] Black Theology must, therefore,

> emerge consciously from an investigation of the socio-religious experience of black people, as that experience is reflected in black stories of God's dealing with black people in the struggle for freedom.[41]

Although differing on how that is to be done, whether through nationalism and the emergence of a separate Black nation (Cleage), by means of a theology which is both liberated, from alienating contexts and understandings, and liberating, in its expression of Black faith in a God who frees physically and spiritually (Cone), or through efforts at a reconciliation between Blacks and whites which acknowledges differences but affirms commonalities (Roberts), for all the truth of Jesus Christ is inseparable from the struggle of the people. It is inseparable from their hopes and their dreams which arise from both the agonies and the defeats of that struggle:

> Truth is that transcendent reality, disclosed in the people's historical struggle for liberation, which enables them to know that their fight for freedom is not futile.[42]

To speak the truth from the Black perspective is to return to the sources of Black Theology: the Black experience as expressed and witnessed in the history and culture of an oppressed but undefeated people. It is first to return to the symbols which have arisen from that experience: God the Omnipresent Creator who has revealed God's love for the oppressed in both the Incarnation of God's Son, Jesus Christ, and acts of liberation throughout human history. The second step then becomes to present those symbols in terms which both shatter reality in this country while at the same time rebuilding and renewing it.

Notes

1. In this decade, works focusing on these specific areas rather than with the broader overviews of the 1970s and 1980s have begun to appear. They include such works as Peter J. Paris, *The Spirituality of African Peoples: The Search for a Common Moral Discourse* (Minneapolis: Augsburg Fortress, 1995), Cheryl J. Sanders, *Living the Intersection: Womanism and Afrocentrism in Theology* (Minneapolis: Augsburg Fortress, 1995); Randall Bailey and Jacqueline Grant, eds., *The Recovery of Black Presence: An Interdisciplinary Exploration* (Nashville: Abingdon Press, 1995), Carlyle Fielding Stewart III, *African American Church Growth* (Nashville: Abingdon Press, 1995), and Julian Kunnie, *Models of Black Theology: Issues in Class, Culture, and Gender* (Valley Forge, Pa.: Trinity Press International, 1994), among others; womanist theological contributions will be discussed in Chapter Seven.

2. Cone, *God of the Oppressed*, Chapter 6, esp. pp. 133-137.

3. Loretta Dornisch, "Symbolic Systems and the Interpretation of Scripture," *Semeia* 4 (1975), p. 7, a discussion of the work of Paul Ricouer.

4. *Black Preaching* (Philadelphia: Lippincott, 1970), p. 27.

5. *Black Religion and Black Radicalism*, p. 237.

6. Wilmore, op. cit.; Mitchell, op. cit.

7. It should be noted here that for Cone and most Black Christians, there is no critical distinction made in speaking about God or Christ. The two words are interchangeable, for they serve as symbols of the Otherness which is present in their lives and which has nurtured them and carried them on.

God is the Being—both immanent and transcendent—who partakes freely in human history by siding with the oppressed in their struggle for freedom. God is Father and Mother, Omnipotent and Omniscient, All-Loving and All-Caring. Jesus Christ is the Incarnation of that love and the manifestation of God's solidarity with the victims. He is Brother, Son and Friend, present here and now in their lives. Christ expresses for most Black Christians who God is in their everyday lives. Thus, in this work, I will use, as Cone does, God/Christ almost interchangeably. The best example of this practice is in *God of the Oppressed* which contains no specific chapter on God as such but deals extensively with the Christ and his importance in the lives of the Black people today. Further discussion of this is presented in Kelly Brown Douglass, *The Black Christ* (Maryknoll: Orbis, 1994); also see Carter, *Prayer Tradition*, p. 50.

8. James H. Cone, *A Black Theology of Liberation* (New York; J.B. Lippincott Co. (1970), reissued, Maryknoll, N.Y.: Orbis Books, 1984), p. 76.

9. Cummings, "Coming Through 'Ligion,'" in *Cut Loose*, p. 86. Also see Johnson, *God Struck Me Dead*.

10. Hopkins, "Slave Theology," op. cit., p. 229.

11. See Cone, *The Spirituals and the Blues*, Hopkins, *Shoes That Fit Our Feet*, Harold Carter, *Prayer Tradition*, Zora Neale Hurston, *The Sanctified Church*, ed. by Toni Cade Bambara (Berkeley: Turtle Island Foundation, 1981), *Mules and Men* (Philadelphia: J.B. Lippincott, 1935; republished 1990, New York: Harper and Row) and *Tell My Horse* (Philadelphia: J.B. Lippincott, 1938; republished 1990, New York: Harper and Row), *The People Could Fly: American Black Folktales* told by Virginia Hamilton (New York: Alfred P. Knopf, 1985) and Roger D. Abrahams, ed., *Afro-American Folk Tales: Stories From Black Traditions in the New World* (N.Y.: Pantheon Books, 1985).

12. *The Spirituals and the Blues*, pp. 30-31.

13. "Slave Theology in the 'Invisible Institution,'" in *Cut Loose Your Stammering Tongue*, pp. 8-9; also see his *Shoes That Fit Our Feet*, chapter 1.

14. See Hopkins, *Shoes*, chapter 1.

15. James H. Cone, *For My People*, pp. 32-33.

16. Elizabeth Johnson, *She Who Is: The Mystery of God in Feminist Theological Discourse* (New York: The Crossroad Publishing Company, 1992), pp. 65-66.

17. Ibid., p. 65.

18. See Cone, *A Black Theology of Liberation*, 2nd ed., chapter 4.

19. Ibid.

20. In his *Is God a White Racist?: A Preamble to Black Theology* (Garden City, NY: Anchor Press/Doubleday, 1973), Jones raises the issue of theodicy and questions Blacks' continued faith in a God who, he asserts, has *not* been seen to act, in any significant way, on their behalf. He calls instead for a humanism which places Black humanity at the decisive center of the struggle for liberation; they are the actors, not God.

21. James H. Cone, *A God of the Oppressed*, p. 35.

22. Ibid., pp. 35-36.

23. As noted in Chapter One, note 22, a similar assertion, couched in the language of its time, was first made by the AME Bishop, Henry McNeale Turner, in 1898 that "God is a Negro." Cone was the first to reassert this in the twentieth century.

24. Ricouer, "Biblical Hermeneutics," *Semeia* 13 (1975) 29-148, p. 79.

25. Ibid., p. 80.

26. James H. Cone, *Black Theology and Black Power*, p. 213.

27. Ibid., p. 216.

28. Ibid., pp. 25-26.

29. Ibid.

30. Avery Dulles, *Models of Revelation* (Garden City: Double-day, 1983; first published by Harper and Row, 1957), p. 46. Also see Paul Tillich, *Dynamics of Faith* (New York: Harper and Row, 1957).

31. Cone, *Black Theology*, p. 27.

32. Ricouer, "Biblical Hermeneutics," p. 84.

33. Ibid., p. 85.

34. Hopkins, *Black Theology: USA and South Africa*, p. 38. In chapters 2 and 3 of this work, Hopkins gives an excellent overview of the major Black theologians (male) who were active in the beginnings of Black Theology. Much of my discussion will be based on his analysis.

35. As quoted in Hopkins, *Black Theology*, Ibid.

36. See his *The Black Messiah* (Kansas City: Sheed, Andrews and McMeel, 1968) and *Black Christian Nationalism: New Directions for the Black Church* (New York: Morrow, 1972). Branches of the Shrine are located in Atlanta, Ga., Houston, Tx. and Detroit, Mi.

37. See Hopkins, *Black Theology*, p. 49.

38. See Roberts, *Liberation and Reconciliation: A Black Theology* (Philadelphia: Westminster Press, 1971; republished, rev. ed. Maryknoll: Orbis, 1994).

39. Hopkins, op. cit., p. 50.

40. This is why a variety of programs on ministry within the Black community have emerged, especially within Christian denominations that are predominantly white with an accompanying lack of sufficient numbers of Black ministers. These programs are an effort to inculturate the Christian message and non-black ministers into the culture of African Americans so that they can, in turn, empower Black Americans to become leaders in their own right while at the same time enabling the non-Black ministers to learn of Black culture while also recognizing that they can never be fully a part of that culture nor can they co-opt it for their own purposes, whether innocent or not.

41. Cone, *God of the Oppressed*, p. 16.

42. Ibid., p. 17.

6

Narrative and Testimony in Black Liberation Theology

It is in the narrative (story) that the symbol and metaphor of God/Christ come together most significantly for Black Theology. Here the historical experience of American Blacks as revealed in the narrative, both oral and written, of Black lives over four hundred years lays the basis for an ecclesiology and eschatology which are both an affirmation of faith and a proclamation of hope.

Narrative is a form of discourse developed in the form of a story which is presented to a public as a reflection on past events, whether real or imaginary. Narrative opens up a new perspective on life and on the future while, at the same time, it represents the nature of the temporality of human existence.[1] Historical narrative, in particular, is grounded in history which presents a "truth-claim" that becomes involved with and ruled by a particular world-view. It is "interested" communication because it is done from a particular perspective, with a particular ideology and commitment. As Dwight Hopkins states in *Cut Loose Your Stammering Tongue*: "Slaves don't stammer; they speak God's truth."[2]

The narratives of slaves and ex-slaves in the USA provide foundational elements for the creation of a constructive black theology of liberation. The religious voices and thoughts of African American chattel do not, however, operate in a passive, non-initiating matter. As a living source and a medium of God's word in action, they compel black theology to deepen further its reliance on indigenous resources in the African American church and community, thereby commanding black theology to cut loose its stammering tongue…. [T]he slaves' faithful story about freedom helps to unleash the full power of African American speech, which reflects and plumbs the depths of God's grace of freedom to the black poor.[3]

All history is about something or someone, an achievement or, rarely, a failure in the lives of particular groups as they live, work and play together in the community, society, and nation.[4] History is usually the story of the conquerors or victors while that of the defeated fades or is erased from memory. Thus, the truth revealed in the Swahili proverb: "One who knows not one's origin is doomed to servitude."[5]

The more I read about black history, the more I became proud that I was black…. A person without a past is a person without an identity. And the absence of an identity is very serious, because without self-knowledge others can make you become what they desire. When that insight was revealed to me, I also realized why whites omitted black people's contributions to humankind in their writing and teaching and in both secular and religious subjects. That was and is their way of making us think we are nothing. To be nothing means that you cannot think. Therefore others must think for you and organize the society without your participation in the organization.[6]

Black Theology is a narrative which seeks to transform this meaning by relating and, thereby, reclaiming and preserving the history of a supposedly vanquished people who paradoxically have survived slavery, discrimination and on-going oppression. Their story is not one of unparalleled success but of continued struggle against frightful odds, of persistence in the face of overwhelming pressures, of faith where all reason had fled.

Just as all theology is contextual, "God-talk," rooted in the particular encounter of a people with their God throughout history, the story of a people's life in this world, is contextual as well.

> Theological problems are not given by divine fiat, nor are theologians' solutions derived only from fixed divine revelation. Theological problems arise from theologians' interests, the issues that they consider important in the definition of their discipline. To *whom* theologians talk and *what* they talk about is a *choice* that they make so as to concretize what is regarded as theology. Therefore, one knows what is important for theologians by whom they talk to and by what they choose to talk about. The issues that define the work of theology define theology itself.
>
> ...the social location and interests of theologians must be critically evaluated in order to understand why they do theology the way they do, and why they advocate certain views and not others.[7]

Black theologians present a "truth-claim" which is Black, one grounded in the experience of Black people in the United States. They speak to, for, and about Black people and that experience in their theology. Their narration, therefore, is the telling of a particular course of events which have special meaning to a particular people. As such, these events can and do impact upon the world in which they evolved, a world which, however, has also conspired to restrict both that evolution and knowledge of it. It is a Black truth, a transcendent reality which fuels the struggle for liberation, one "disclosed in the history and culture of black people."[8]

> ...the essence of black religion is expressed in the form of story. By telling the story of African American faith, the past is preserved and kept alive in the collective memory of the community, the enigmas and puzzles of contemporary life are demystified, and the future is suggestively inferred and hinted at. Moreover, a genuine story initiates some kind of transformation in the life of the hearer and requires a response to its truth.[9]

It is the story of how African peoples were brought to this country, why they were brought, and what happened to them once they arrived which is the context for Black Theology. It is the history of:

> ...every conceivable method used to destroy black humanity. But it is also the history of blacks' refusal to acquiesce in their destruction. It is also the story of God's dealings with black people in the struggle for freedom. Thus, it reveals the true meaning of God to and for blacks and the meaning of his Son who is the eternal event of liberation in the divine person who makes freedom a constituent of human existence.[10]

This narrative has served as both a goad to further effort and a solace in times of need, which has called Blacks forth to continue to build upon the foundation provided them by their foremothers and forefathers. As stated above, symbols both are influenced by developing world-views and also influence those views. Therefore, it is precisely because the world-views of Black Americans and white Americans are, for the most part, at odds with each other that the significance of Black Theology can be seen in its narration of the story of a people whose history and very existence has been ignored, denied and rendered marginal for centuries in the United States. Black Theology reveals a different way of thinking, one which views the world from the eyes of those on the "underside of history," those with no one to turn to but God, rather than from the eyes of the oppressors, who too often have mistaken themselves for God. An example of the latter perspective is presented by Hopkins:

> ...even if slave masters granted any possibility of slaves attaining the blessed repose of heaven, they had to beseech the white man as their Savior. For example, a slave master caught his slave praying and demanded that the slave explain to whom he offered supplications. The slave replied: 'Oh Marster, I'se just prayin' to Jesus 'cause I wants to go to Heaven when I dies.' Belligerently and arrogantly, the Marster replied, 'You's my Negro. I get ye to Heaven.' Here we touch the heart of white Christianity and theology. The white man believed he filled the mediating and liberating role of Jesus Christ. As the anointed Jesus, the white man possessed omnipotent and salvific capabilities. For black chattel to reach God, then, whites forced African Americans to accept the status of the white race as divine mediator.[11]

Clearly, it is not possible for Black and white Americans to have the same views about God/Christ because their situations in and experiences of life have been so drastically opposite.

The story of the Black experience is one that catches our interest and holds it, for it is the classic narrative of the weak overcoming the strong. Yet, it is also a story which is still being told, a conclusion that has, as yet, not been written but is being lived out in the daily existence of the Black community and personified in its religious faith.

African-American religion is not a static phenomenon, but is the result of a dynamic interaction of the remembered past, the experienced present, and the anticipated future. It reflects the changeable character of African American experience in the world. Even the form of black religion, then, must suit the variable spiritual, emotional, and physical needs of its adherents.[12]

The Black heritage is presented and is identified as being part of each and every Black person, whether such persons are aware of it or not. Thus, it is history, but a history which involves not only the stories of the past but also those of the present and those yet to be lived, the story of the coming to be of a new people. It is because of the meaning that has been revealed in their history that Blacks have been empowered to go forth into the future. Theirs is a communal destiny, not an individual one. It is as a people, they realize, that they are freed by the narrative of their lives and the lives of those who have gone before them to communicate in the fullest sense, not only with those who are living, but also with the ancestors and those yet to be born. Black history in the United States is, in its fullest understanding, a "subversive memory"[13] which turns all of reality upside down and makes of apparent defeat a continuing victory.

James Evans sees African-American theology, therefore, as "the explanation, defense, and critique of the religious practice and interpretation of the black community." Narrative must, as a consequence of this understanding, be the necessary form of Black Theology because the form of Black religion is story. As such, it reunites the two aspects of human activity separated as a result of Enlightenment thought. Praxis and criticism, faith and reason, are no longer antagonistic but come together to create a new and holistic reality.

Traditional metaphysics is no longer an adequate base for doing theology because it depends on a common vision of "reality as such" and a common notion of "general human experience".... African-American theological narrative is a retelling of the black religious story with an emphasis on intellectual clarity and existential commitment.[14]

The presentation of the Black historical experience in Black Theology thus enlarges our sphere of communication by capturing and presenting to us those values and beliefs from the past which must be remembered, the "subversive memory" of the redemptive suffering of a people, and by distancing our own desires and preoccupations so that we can come to understand what is different about this world which has been revealed to us.

Narrative (the telling and retelling of a people's story) leads to community. It helps to build and sustain community and is, itself, nurtured and given new life by the community. As Alice Walker notes: "The artist is the voice of the people but she is also the people." The community is the source—both in the past and continuing—of the story as it unfolds. It is the community which makes history by living out its day-to-day existences. And it is the Black community which, in so doing, makes up the Black Church.

The Black Community and Church as Testimony

The language of symbol and metaphor as related in Chapter Four and of narrative, as discussed above, finds expression in a witness, a testimony, a faith lived, believed and proclaimed. This is the faith of the Black community which is manifested, in its deepest sense, in the Black Church.

> Testimony applies to those words, works, actions and...
> lives which attest to an intention, an inspiration, an idea
> at the heart of experience and history which nonetheless
> transcends experience and history.[15]

Testimony negates the limitations of individual destiny. It is both statement and belief. It is the act of testifying and the story of the event which is being testified to. Testimony is both a category which refers back to the problem of evil and finitude and is itself a symbol. It thus serves as affirmation while offering in hope, while, at the same time, by occurring in the context of trial and judgment, it engages the commitment and credibility of the witness in the Black community. It is the living testimony of how Blacks have been and continue to be able to survive.

This is why for Gayraud Wilmore, "the first source of black theology is the community itself" which is both a part of and often apart from the Black Church as an institutional entity.[16] He asserts that it is the Black community which serves as the font for numerous groups active in Black society today. These groups, whether part of or apart from the institutional Church as such, will continue to be viable, however, only as long as they maintain their roots in that community, especially in the lower-class Black community.

> Black theologians must learn to appreciate and under-
> stand these roots before turning to white scholars for the
> substance of their reflection on the meaning of God,
> human existence, and freedom. Folk religion is a
> constituent factor in every significant crisis in the black
> community. We ignore it only at the risk of being cut off
> from the real springs of action.[17]

While recognizing the importance of Black secular institutions, for James Cone it is the church itself, the embodiment of the Black Christian community, which has been and continues to be most significant for the continuation and delineation of the Black story and, therefore, Black Theology. The Black Church, for Cone, serves as a challenge to the racism of the institutional Church. It is more than buildings, institution or hierarchy; it is the living body of Christ which exists to transform the world, which speaks to African Americans in their state of oppression and marginalization in the United States.

> The black church was the creation of a black people whose daily existence was an encounter with the overwhelming and brutalizing reality of white power. For the slaves it was the sole source of personal identity and the sense of community.[18]

The Black Church also gave witness to the "loss" of faith which the Black community suffered in the late nineteenth and early twentieth centuries. That period in time was witness to the decline of a Church formed as a result of Black people's denial of a restrictive white interpretation of God for them to a Church which gradually became co-opted by the same white institutional Churches from which they had originally departed. Although by so doing, the Churches may have, to a certain extent, protected the lives of their people from the life-threatening effects of racism, in so doing they also lost contact with that liberating God they had formerly proclaimed and which had been a source of their survival.

The true role of the Church, as witness to God's revelation in Christ as the liberator of the oppressed and downtrodden, is to take action, concrete action, on their behalf. For Cone, it is no longer a haven of safety but a radical sign of contradiction as Christ himself was. Its role is to be totally involved in and accepting of the role of co-sufferer with its people, while at the same time challenging that "victimhood" in order to replace it with a church and people who have overcome their suffering and are claiming empowered roles in today's society.

To be a Christian Church, Cone asserts, is to be an instrument of freedom. Justice's struggle must be a requirement for true Christian being. The Church must become politically involved. It must become one in solidarity with the victims, balancing its theology with its praxis or better, reforming and continually refining its theology by its praxis in the world and by its actions transforming alleged "victims" into true "victors."

Albert Cleage would agree with Cone in part. He sees the Black Church as the "initiator" of Black liberation which will lead to the eventual emergence of a Black nation. Cleage, therefore, attacks the Black Church for "incorrectly nurturing a gospel of salvation instead of a gospel of liberation." The goal of his liberation ecclesiology is "an immediate, earthly kingdom in the form of a black nation within the over-all American white nation."[19] The Church, in his understanding, serves as the power base for this nation.

> Our basic task is bringing black people together and building a Nation. This church [the Shrine of the Black Madonna] is the hub of the emerging Black Nation. From it we go out in all directions to educate, to set up action centers.[20]

The other theologians discussed herein would not go this far. While recognizing the importance of and necessity for a vital and active Black Church grounded in the community of believers which serves as a catalyst for transformation of Black reality, they would balk at Cleage's conclusion that the necessary outcome of that transformation is an independent Black nation. They seek both to uplift and sustain the Black community while, at the same time, sounding a note of warning coupled with a desire for mutual reconciliation based on a viable and true equality of peoples.

The Church is a mission in and of itself. It is and must be the model for the outreach which is incumbent upon all Christians, whatever their race. The Church cannot serve merely as a "service station" where one goes to fill up on the Holy Spirit when one is running low. That time has passed, if it should ever have existed. The Church must be, and is, a witness to the reality, painful as it may be, of what went on before and what is going on now and what is yet to come in the lives of Black Americans and, therefore, in the life of all Americans.

It is the people themselves who are the very heart of the Church. It is their testimony and the witness of their lives that has brought it into being. Calling to mind once again the Black Catholic Bishops' recognition that the Black Church is an entity which crosses denominational lines to form a community of peoples who share in communal prayer and Christian action, this reality, however, brings with it a challenge: "The unique context and the array of traditions, customs, and styles within African-American Christianity make the formulation of a black ecclesiology difficult." A further challenge is "that the notion of community is so basic to African-American religious experience that the normal doctrinal explanations for church formation are not sufficient."[21] At the same time, Black Christians must overcome their own internal prejudices which have, too often, separated Protestant from Catholic, middle class from lower class and those whose African ancestors were set down in other lands before eventually making their way to the United States.

> ...the African-American cultural heritage is vast and rich.
> The cultural idiom of American Black people has never
> been uniform but has varied according to region and
> ethos. African, Haitian, Latin and West Indian cultural
> expressions also contribute to this day to nurture the
> Black American cultural expression.[22]

Acknowledgment and acceptance of this reality is a
necessity for continued black survival as a people. Black
Americans must rebuild their communities in order to
regain that unity which enabled them to "make it over"
the "rough places and the straight" in the past and to
rebuild the foundation for a viable Black future.

A return to testimony and the narratives, oral and
written, of Black peoples themselves is vital in order to
understand what the full meaning of Church is for them.
Lines of denomination, class and all else must be crossed
in order to see, through their own witness that, despite its
shortcomings and occasional lapses, the Black Church, as
the community of all Black believers in Christ, is still a
focal point, the unyielding ground beneath their feet, a
place of refuge and strength which helps them to both
recuperate from and prepare for the battles to come.

We are thus brought back once again to the acknowledgment that two traditions, survival and liberation, do
indeed exist in Black religion. The Black Church harbors
and nurtures both poles within itself, presenting one
face or the other, at the time most appropriate as guided,
one could argue, by the Holy Spirit.[23] This is why, as
Wilmore asserts, that,

> the black church...is at once the most reactionary and
> the most radical of black institutions; the most imbued
> with the mythology and values of white America, and yet
> the most proud, the most independent and indigenous
> collectivity in the black community.

Black pride and power, black nationalism and pan-
Africanism have had no past without the black church
and black religion, and without them may well have no
enduring future.[24]

Thus, even those institutions and ideologies which seem
to be furthest in their praxis and understanding from
the Church can be seen to be, in actuality, deeply rooted
in it.

The death of Jesus is also a testimony, for he is both
accuser and accused of the people, condemned and
vindicated by the people. Jesus' death is a testimony of
the evil which can be found in humanity as well as of the
love which can be found both in humanity and in God.
This pivotal death forms the basis for belief by
eyewitnesses and by those who have only heard and, in
hearing, believed and, therefore, also have seen. This is
the religious meaning of testimony. The one witnessing
is the one commissioned to testify. He or she does not
testify regarding isolated contingent fact but about the
radical, global meaning of human experience. The
testimony is oriented toward proclamation, divulging,
propagation; and it implies a total engagement not only
of word but of deed.

Such testimony is a revelation of the Absolute, for it is
not that of the witness but that of the Other. It is a
revelation for all people given in one people. Thus, as the
Israelites confessed Yahweh initially by confessing their
own deliverance, so Blacks confess God in the language
of their own liberation, first from a similar enslavement
and, in time, from all forms of enslavement. One who
witnesses to the Absolute can do so only by witnessing to
the historic signs, the acts of deliverance as they took
place and continue to take place in history. Thus, it is in
the liberative acts of God in their own history that Black

Americans have seen and having seen are empowered to testify to God's meaning in their lives. And it is in those liberative acts of God in their own history that they have come to recognize God as "Black" in solidarity with their blackness.

The question is continually raised in liberation theology: Does any group or people have the right to invest a moment of history with an absolute character?[25] Black theologians, male and female, Protestant and Catholic, would answer yes. For what is involved in testimony and its interpretation is the search for original affirmation and absolute knowledge in human consciousness itself, on which it serves as a judgment.[26]

The story (narrative) of Black people which reveals the liberating acts of God/Christ throughout their experience is a witness against, if not a judgment upon, white America. For in their suffering and dying, Blacks have been the witnesses who

> seal [their] bond to the cause that [they] defend by a public profession of their conviction, by the zeal of a propagator, by a personal devotion which can extend even to the sacrifice of...life. The witness is capable of suffering and dying for what he believes.[27]

Blacks serve as witness and judge, as proclaimer of truth and convicter of falsity, as victim (judged) and victor (judge). It is this paradox which gives way to their hope and is the foundation for their continuing faith.

God/Christ, therefore, is the event, above all others, who manifests the divine self in the events of history. Divine interventions in history are historical facts which form the basis not only for revelation but for proclaiming that revelation. In order to understand the otherness of the event which is God/Christ, it must be placed into an historical framework.

The Exodus story, and the stories of the life, death and resurrection of Jesus Christ and of the emancipation of African Americans, are the events, par excellence, revelatory of God's nature. The temporality of these events is not limited or exhausted at the time they took place; rather, they "remain an event of hope as the future of the fulfillment of the promise."[28]

It is precisely the resurrection of Jesus as future which determines the Black person's future as a possibility independent of his or her own decision or power. The event is eschatological in character:

> ...black people are now free to be for the black community, to make decisions about their existence in the world without an undue preoccupation with white ideas about "odds" (we have all the guns) or victory (you cannot win). Ultimately (and this is what God's transcendence means) black humanity is not dependent on our power to win.[29]

Black Hope

In the end, the formulation of a theological system which explicates the Black contention that God/Christ is with, for, and one with Black people is revealed. It is the symbol (God/Christ) which participates in making up the metaphor (God/Christ as Black) which in itself becomes part of a narrative (the Black story), which is testimony to a faith in God/Christ, and which creates the beings who profess that faith (the Black Church and community). The Word of God erupts into Black lives and transforms them, creating new beings able to reflect on the experience which is given them in God's Word. That Word, for African Americans, is the Word of freedom and of liberation; it is the proclamation that God, in the form of Jesus Christ, has come specifically to free those enslaved. It comes in the form of kerygma, which is hope, a hope founded/grounded in God's liberating Word. God's Word is a poetic happening, an evocation of an indescribable reality in the lives of people. It is the embodiment of freedom.

It is a Word of hope which must be proclaimed. The story must be told. The basis for the hope must be preached to all so that all may hear and be transformed by the "Good News." However, in the proclaiming of that hope, there also lies the responsibility of living it, in true not token solidarity with those who are oppressed. It is not a hope merely to be listened to but one which acts to transform those who hear the Word of God and believe. The task of the Church, therefore, of necessity is to proclaim that hope and to live it in witness to the coming of the Kingdom.

Black theology, in all of its manifestations, speaks a "passionate language" because it is a "survival" theology, one which translates into hope for the future. It is a theology committed in hope, a hope which it preaches as a revolutionary hope, a hope which overthrows the powers and principalities of this world in favor of those who are unwanted, unthought of, unloved.

The hope which is preached is the hope of the Black community. It is the power which formed them and which keeps them alive today. Black hope gives Black people the courage to be themselves, to live their own lives and to rejoice in that living.

It is a hope which is alive, which is on-going, ever-active, ever-becoming. It is a hope that "proclaims a yes to history as the primary focus of the manifestation of hope, but, at the same time, a no to any attempt to equate the movement of history with totality."[30] Thus, the kingdom is "here but not yet." It is not fully realized because humanity is itself finite, yet the Spirit of the Lord is working within God's people to enable them to overthrow the shackles of poverty and oppression and to work for freedom and justice in this world, as well as toward a freedom and justice which will not be totally fulfilled until Christ comes again.

It is an interpreted hope, one necessarily grounded in the faith and texts of the Judeo-Christian tradition, in the texts of Sacred Scripture. To begin aright is to begin, not with theological propositions, but from the source of those propositions, and it is that source which is "the most originary expression of a community of faith."[31] Each community must return to that source, to explore and interpret its meaning for itself out of its own lived experience of God's revelatory events in its life. Thus, Black Theology must uncover "the structures and forms of the black experience because the categories of interpretations must arise out of the thought forms of the black experience itself."[32]

This is what Black theologians have attempted to do in diverse ways. They explore the use of certain forms of language as they arise out of the Black context. It can be said that they have taken the bare bones of a hermeneutic of symbol, metaphor, narrative, and testimony and enfleshed them, like Elijah, with the lives and voices of a particular people, an oppressed people, who, in the working out and coming to be of their own existence and their reality, have breathed new life into what was thought dead and, in so doing, have transformed the abstractness of theory into the embodiment of praxis.

However, they have done so relying on only one perspective for the most part, that of Black Protestant males. The following two chapters will present and develop the voices of Black women and Black Catholics.

Notes

1. John W. Van den Hengel, *The Home of Meaning: The Hermeneutic of the Subject of Paul Ricouer* (Washington, D.C.: University Press of America 1982), pp. 134-146.

2. "Introduction," p. xvi.

3. Ibid., pp. xv-xvi.

4. Ricouer, "The Narrative Function," *Semeia* 13 (1978), p. 182.

5. Cited in Gay Wilentz, *Binding Cultures: Black Women Writers in Africa and the Diaspora* (Bloomington: Indiana University Press, 1992), p. 116.

6. James Cone, *My Soul Looks Back* (Nashville: Abingdon, 1982, Journeys of Faith series, Robert A. Raines, ed.), p. 28.

7. Cone, *For My People*, p. 29.

8. Cone, *God of the Oppressed*, p. 17.

9. Evans, *We Have Been Believers*, p. 24.

10. Ibid., pp. 34-35.

11. "Slave Theology in the 'Invisible Institution'," in *Cut Loose*, p. 12. The narrative quoted by Hopkins is from Norman R. Yetman, *Life Under the "Peculiar Institution": Selections from the Slave Narrative Collection* (New York: Holt, Rinehart and Winston, 1970), pp. 231-232. He also recommends reviewing Levine, *Black Culture*, pp. 41-42, 46 and Charles L. Perdue, Jr., et al., eds., *Weevils in the Wheat: Interviews with Virginia Ex-Slaves* (Bloomington: Indiana University Press, 1980; originally published by the University Press of Virginia in 1976), pp. 207, 290.

12. Evans, *Believers*, p. 24.

13. See Johann Baptist Metz, *Faith in History and Society,*

and Hayes, "Tracings of an American Theology," in *Louvain Studies* 14/4 (Winter 1989).

14. Evans, pp. 24-25.

15. Ricouer, "The Hermeneutics of Testimony," in Lewis S. Mudge (ed.), *Essays on Biblical Interpretation* (Philadelphia: Fortress Press, 1980), p. 119.

16. Wilmore, *Black Religion*, p. 235.

17. Ibid.

18. Cone, *Black Theology and Black Power*, p. 92.

19. Hopkins, *Black Theology*, p. 39.

20. See *The Black Messiah*, p. 277, and *Black Christian Nationalism*, p. 232.

21. Evans, *Believers*, p. 120.

22. *What We Have Seen and Heard*, p. 31.

23. Wilmore, *Black Religion*, pp. 227ff.

24. Ibid., p. x.

25. Ricouer, "The Hermeneutics of Testimony," p. 142.

26. Ibid., p. 154.

27. Ibid., p. 129.

28. Van den Hengel, p. 225.

29. Cone, *A Black Theology of Liberation*, p. 143.

30. Van den Hengel, p. 228.

31. Ibid., p. 229.

32. Cone, *A Black Theology of Liberation*, p. 51.

7

The Vision of Black Women: Womanist Theology

        Black Liberation Theology in the United States has been seen for the most part as a product of the Black Protestant Church and community. The leading scholars in the field have been Black men, most of whom have been ordained to the ministry in the historically Black Methodist or Baptist Churches. It is only in the last fifteen or so years that Black women, also predominantly Protestant, have become part of the dialogue. The reasons for this are rather obvious.[1]

Black women, whether Protestant or Catholic, while the mainstay, as all women have been, of the Christian Churches, have held few significant roles of responsibility or leadership within them, especially as ordained ministers. Those who did have such roles, few as they were, were constantly challenged by both men and women as to the propriety of their roles, their ability to fulfill them, and the validity of their calling.[2] Today, this situation is slowly changing in the Protestant Churches as women enter programs of theological study in ever increasing numbers.[3]

In an age of liberation movements, women have been

the unheard voices calling for recognition and the freedom to speak of their lives in words of their own choosing. Women of color have especially suffered from the oppression of others, both male and female, speaking for and about them.[4]

In this chapter, I will briefly address some of the historical reasons behind the failure to address the issues of women of color, particularly Black women, in the feminist and Black Theology movements as well as present the thought of the womanist theological movement which provides a needful critique of both.

The Triple Oppression of Black Women

Zora Neale Hurston depicted the condition of African American women with a starkness still relevant today in *Their Eyes Were Watching God*.[5] The grandmother, Nanny, reflecting on her own experience of the world, tells Janie, her granddaughter, that "De nigger woman is de mule uh de world so far as Ah can see. Ah been praying fuh it to be different wid you."[6] And so Black mothers have been praying since Blacks were first forcibly introduced to the United States as an enslaved and dehumanized people.

A significant result of that introduction was the development of a mythology which continues to the present day to alienate Black and white women as well as Black women and black men: the myth of "white womanhood."[6a] An integral part of this myth is the polarized depictions of Black and white women in which the latter retain all of the allegedly positive feminine characteristics: gentle, nurturing, sensitive, intuitive, helpless, dependent, which serve to place white women on a pedestal, while the former, given the allegedly negative feminine attributes: temptress, promiscuous, independent, unnatural mother, are seen as the lowest depths of humanity or, usually, outside of humanity entirely. A black woman was all that a white woman should not be. She was, indeed, seen as the "mule" of American society by all, oftentimes even by herself, forced to bear burdens the lowest animal was not required to bear, and denounced for the very degradation forced upon her.

The following is a typical view stated by a white Southern woman in a public newspaper in 1904:

> Negro women evidence more nearly the popular idea of total depravity than the men do.... When a man's mother, wife and daughters are all immoral women, there is no room in his fallen nature for the aspiration of honor and virtue.... I cannot imagine such a creation as a virtuous black woman.[7]

Sojourner Truth's challenging cry, "Ain't I a woman?" pointed out, however, the lie within this misidentification, one which enabled white women to claim a "victimhood" in common with Black women, a victimhood which existed in name only rather than in actual shared denigration and oppression.[8] It was often argued that the "physical assaults against black women in slavery; as well as the psychological deprivation resulting from their loss of control of their own persons," could be equated "with the white slave mistresses' psychological pain at their husbands' behavior."[9] Yet, as Linda Brent, herself a slave, wrote of her white mistress:

> I was soon convinced that her emotions arose more from anger and wounded pride. She felt that her marriage vows were desecrated, her dignity insulted; but she had no compassion for the poor victims of her husband's perfidy. She pitied herself as a martyr; but she was incapable of feeling for the condition of shame and misery in which her unfortunate helpless slaves were placed.[10]

Rather than being treated with kindness and compassion, the raped slave woman was all too often treated harshly, beaten to the point of death, and her child sold away from her, at the order of her enraged and "violated" mistress.[11]

It is this seeming blindness toward the inequitable positions of both Black and white women which continues to serve as a barrier to concerted action on the part of many feminists of different races today. For the feminist movement, both politically and theologically, has, historically, been one of white women, usually educated, middle- and upper-class women, with the freedom and privilege to become militant without fearing consequences as harsh as those a Black woman or working class white women would be subjected to. In the Roman Catholic Church, especially, the greater number of women advocating equality have been women religious with similar education, freedoms and privileges. The result has been that the experience of white women has been presented as universal, incorporating and speaking for the experience of all women. It is not that women of color are assumed to be incapable of speaking for themselves; rather, their silence or absence is, simply, not even noted or seen as represented by a token few.

Many Black women have critical concerns about the feminist movement and, therefore, with feminist theology. This is only partly due to the often distorted images received from the media, the Christian Churches and other sources. Rather, Black women assert that they are unable to identify with either the movement or its theological expression because the agendas are so different from their own, failing to fully address the myriad issues of class and race as well as gender with which they are beset.[12]

Many women are reluctant to advocate feminism because they are uncertain about the meaning of the term. Other women from exploited and oppressed ethnic groups dismiss the term because they do not wish to be perceived as supporting a racist movement; feminism is often equated with white women's rights effort. Large numbers of women see feminism as synonymous with lesbianism; their homophobia leads them to reject association with any group identified as pro-lesbian. Some women fear the word "feminism" because they shun identification with any political movement, especially one perceived as radical. Of course there are women who do not wish to be associated with [the] women's rights movement in any form, so they reject and oppose the feminist movement.[13]

Recognizing these differences, Black women assert their need for the freedom and space to empower themselves and to engage in their own efforts at consciousness-raising as well as to share those efforts with others, both male and female. Patricia Hill Collins affirms this necessity in presenting the context for her work on Black feminist consciousness:

I place Black women's experience and ideas at the center of analysis.... I have deliberately chosen not to begin with feminist tenets developed from the experiences of white, middle-class, Western women and then insert the ideas and experiences of African-American women.... Oppressed groups are frequently placed in the situation of being listened to only if we frame our ideas in the language that is familiar to and comfortable for a dominant group. This requirement often changes the meaning of our ideas and works to elevate the ideas of dominant groups.[14]

As Collins privileges the ideas of African American women in the social and political realm, womanist theologians are doing the same in theological circles. By doing so, Black feminists and womanist theologians "encourage white feminists, African-American men, and all others to investigate the similarities and differences among their own standpoints and those of African-American women."[15]

The Development of Womanist Theology

A womanist, as Alice Walker has defined the term, is a Black feminist or feminist of color. She is one "wanting to know more and in greater depth than is good for one.... [She is] outrageous, audacious, courageous and [engages in] willful behavior."[16] A womanist is universal, encompassing love for men and women, as well as music, dance, food, roundness, the struggle, the Spirit and herself, "regardless." She is "committed to survival and wholeness of an entire people, male and female" and is opposed to separation, "except for health."[17]

A womanist sees herself both individually and in community, but that individuality, in keeping with her wholistic African heritage, arises from the community in which she is born, shaped and formed. Her goal of liberation, therefore, which is both spiritual and physical, is not simply for herself but for all of her people and, beyond that, for all who are also oppressed by reason of race, sex, and/or class. Sexism is not the only issue; rarely is it the most important issue. Rather, it is the intertwined evils emanating from and the multiplicative effect of all of these which act to restrict her and her community that are the cause for her concern. Thus, womanism, in an inclusive sense, can be seen as encompassing a more limited feminism in its openness to all who are oppressed for whatever reason.

This understanding has been taken up by Black women theologians, both Protestant, such as Dolores Williams,[18] Jacquelyn Grant,[19] Katie Cannon,[20] Emilie Townes,[21] Renita Weems,[22] Cheryl Saunders[23] and Kelly Brown Douglas,[24] and Catholic, including Shawn Copeland, Jamie Phelps, Toinette Eugene,[25] Diana L. Hayes[26] and other Black women who have attempted to broaden that definition and invest it with a theological and spiritual interpretation which is proving to be emancipatory for many.

Womanist theologians take issue with the perspectives of both white feminist theology and Black male liberation theology. Both can be seen as engaging in "God-talk" from a too narrowly particular and exclusive context. Both err, as noted above and in Chapter Three, in seeing their own particular experiences as the norm for all theologizing. Womanist theology, however, insists that full human liberation can only be achieved by the elimination, not of only one form of oppression, but of all.

As white women can be both oppressor and oppressed, oppressor in their behavior toward women of color or lower class women while at the same time being oppressed by a male-dominated patriarchal society, Black men also occupy the dualistic roles of oppressor of women, especially Black women, and oppressed as Black men. This too often leaves the Black woman on the bottom, as Hurston noted, stigmatized and condemned both for her strengths and her weaknesses and too often denied a space of her own in which to grow, explore and develop into full womanhood. It also leaves her, paradoxically, with a challenging freedom which, however, can also prove dangerous. She has "a lived experience that directly challenges the prevailing classist, sexist, racist social structure and its concomitant ideology"[27] but, at the same time, must herself be careful not to consider herself thereby free of the temptation to sin against others as well in other ways.[28]

This paradoxical existence provides Black women with a consciousness that enables them to critique the persistent evils still prevailing both in United States society and in the Christian churches of the United States, as well as to provide a voice that can enrich the debate on liberation and a praxis that models it.

Womanist Voices

Womanist theologians present a strong rebuttal to the depiction of Black women as the "mule of the world" as Hurston herself did in her many writings which provide a "concrete frame of reference for understanding the Black woman as a moral agent."[29] As Katie Cannon notes, "Hurston's own beingness is both the subject and object of her work." In that work, Black life, as a whole, was seen "as psychologically integral—not mutilated half-lives, stunted by the effects of racism and poverty. She simply could not depict blacks as defeated, humiliated, degraded, or victimized, because she did not experience black people or herself that way."[30]

Katie Cannon

Cannon, in her groundbreaking work, *Black Womanist Ethics*, relies on the life and works of Zora Neale Hurston to engage in an examination of the "matrix of virtues which emerge from the real-lived texture of the Black community."[31] She goes beyond the boundaries of traditional Protestant ethics which, historically, have implied "that the doing of Christian ethics in the Black community was either immoral or amoral."[32] Rather, she asserts that

> the real-lived texture of Black life requires moral agency that may run contrary to the critical boundaries of mainline Protestantism. Blacks may use action guides which have never been considered within the scope of traditional codes of faithful living. Racism, gender discrimination, and economic exploitation, as inherited, age-long complexes, require the Black community to create and cultivate values and virtues in their own terms so that they can prevail against the odds with moral integrity.[33]

Neither the ethical values nor the ethical assumptions of the Black community are "identical with the body of obligations and duties that Anglo-Protestant American society requires of its membership."[34] Nor can they be, "as long as powerful whites who control the wealth, the systems and the institutions in this society continue to perpetuate brutality and criminality against Blacks."[35]

In her study of the historical context in which Black women find themselves as moral agents, Cannon analyzes the moral situation of Black women in the twentieth century situation arising out of the struggle "to survive in two contradictory worlds simultaneously, 'one white, privileged and oppressive, the other black, exploited and oppressed.'"[36]

In so doing, she walks in the path created by other women before her who sought to define the meaning of Black women's lives and to expand the boundaries of those lives beyond the limited horizons established by both white and Black patriarchal social systems—women such as Harriet Tubman, Sojourner Truth, Jarena Lee, Nannie Helen Burroughs, Margaret Walker, Anna Cooper, Mary McLeod Bethune, Frances

Ellen Watkins Harper, Ida B. Wells Barnett, Mary Church Terrell, Ella Baker, Fannie Lou Hamer: the list goes on, yet most of these women are unknown outside of the Black community and little known even within it.[37]

Like these women, womanist theologians use the "stuff" of women's lives to spin a narrative of their persistent effort to rise above and beyond those persons and situations which attempt to hold them down. Their sources are social, political, anthropological and, especially, literary, seeing, as Cannon does, Black women's literary tradition as a "valid source for the central rubrics of the Black woman's odyssey,"[38] for it is in her literary writings that she sets forth the documentation of the "living out" of Black lives in a world confronted daily by racism, sexism, and poverty.

Dolores Williams

It was Dolores Williams, however, in her article, "Womanist Theology: Black Women's Voices,"[39] who was the first to clearly articulate a womanist perspective in Christian theology. Grounded in and emerging from the definition of the term "womanist" by Alice Walker, as noted above, Williams sets forth the parameters for a womanist theological methodology consisting of "a.) a multidialogical intent, b.) a liturgical intent, c.) a didactic event, and d.) a commitment both to reason and to the validity of female imagery and metaphorical language in the construction of theological statements."[40]

In her development, she asserts:

> (A) multidialogical intent will allow Christian womanist theologians to advocate and participate in dialogue and action with *many* diverse social, political, and religious

communities concerned about human survival and a productive quality of life for the oppressed....

If womanist theological method is informed by a liturgical intent, then womanist theology will be relevant to (and will reflect) the thought, worship, and action of the Black Church. But a liturgical intent will also allow womanist theology to challenge the thought/worship/action of the Black Church with the discordant and prophetic messages emerging from womanist participation in multidialogics.[41]

This intent, then, will enable womanist theology to "consciously impact *critically* upon the foundations of liturgy" providing a serious demand for the incorporation of "justice principles" by which "to select the sources that will share the content of liturgy" and enabling questions regarding the portrayal of "blackness/darkness, women, and economic justice for non-ruling class people" in liturgy.[42]

Next, Williams calls for a "didactic intent" which will "teach Christians new insights about moral life based on ethics supporting justice for women, survival, and a productive quality of life for poor women, children and men."[43] By doing so, she can be said to be in agreement, therefore, with Katie Cannon's designation of the importance of "black women's moral wisdom (expressed in their literature)" and Black folk wisdom as sources for a Black ethic.

Finally, these various intents come together to yield "a theological language whose foundation depends" upon both imagery and reason, resulting in the bringing of "black women's history, culture, and religious experience into the interpretive circle of Christian theology and into the liturgical life of the Church. Womanist theological language (for Williams) must, in this sense, be an instrument for social and theological change in church and society."[44]

As noted, Williams has expanded upon these parameters in her recent work, *Sisters in the Wilderness*, where she expands upon her methodology for a womanist theology. In this work, she raises critical questions regarding the position of women, Black women in particular, in Christian society especially with regard to the consistent emphasis on surrogacy as an aspect of Christian womanhood.

> Two kinds of social-role surrogacy have negatively affected the lives of African-American women and mothers: coerced surrogacy and voluntary surrogacy. Coerced surrogacy, belonging to the ante-bellum period, was a condition in which people and systems more powerful than black people forced black women to function in roles that ordinarily would have been filled by someone else.... Slave women could not exercise the choice of refusing surrogacy roles.
>
> After emancipation, the coercion associated with antebellum surrogacy was replaced by social pressures that influenced many black women to continue to fill some surrogacy roles.... The difference was that black women, after emancipation, could exercise the choice of refusing the surrogate role, but social pressures often influenced the choices black women made as they adjusted to life in a free world. Thus postbellum surrogacy can be referred to as voluntary (though pressured) surrogacy.[45]

Her critique of Anselm's doctrine of salvation via atonement is important for today's world with its growing body of "have-nots" serving involuntarily as surrogate sufferers for a minority of "haves." Williams raises the question: Does the image of a surrogate God (that is, one who died for humanity's sins, whether coerced or voluntarily) have salvific power for Black women—(and, logically, any who are oppressed)—or does this image support and reinforce the exploitation that has accompanied their experience of surrogacy— both during and after slavery? Her answer is an unequivocal no. Just as Anselm and others used the language of the sociopolitical thought of their time to render Christian ideas and principles understandable, so womanist theologians, she asserts,

> are empowered to use the "sociopolitical thought and action of the African American woman's world to show Black women that their salvation does not depend upon any form of surrogacy...rather their survival is assured by Jesus' life of resistance and by the survival strategies he used to help people survive the death of identity caused by their exchange of inherited cultural meanings for a new identity shaped by the gospel ethical and world view."[46]

Jesus came to bring life, not death. Expanding upon this, she notes:

> ...the spirit of God in Jesus came to show humans *life*— to show redemption through a perfect *ministerial* vision of righting relations between body (individual and community), mind (of humans and tradition) and spirit....
>
> God's gift to humans, through Jesus, was to invite them to participate in this *ministerial* vision ('whosoever will, let them come') of righting relations....
>
> ...Humankind is, then, redeemed through Jesus' *ministerial* vision of life and not through his death. There is nothing divine in the blood of the cross. God does not intend Black women's surrogacy experience. Neither can Christian faith affirm such an idea. Jesus did not come to be a surrogate. Jesus came for life, to show humans a perfect vision of ministerial relation that humans had very little knowledge of. As Christians, Black women

cannot forget the cross, but neither can they glorify it. To do so is to glorify suffering and to render their exploitation sacred. To do so is to glorify the sin of defilement.[47]

Williams clearly throws down a gauntlet which cannot be ignored. The question of surrogate suffering and its consistent application to women and other marginalized peoples is one which requires further critical dialogue. The rephrasing of this question from the perspective of Black women presents it in a radically different light.

Other womanist theologians, both Protestant and Catholic, are raising equally critical questions and presenting them to the patriarchal and Eurocentric academic and ecclesial worlds, demanding their inclusion in the ongoing religious dialogue.[48]

Jacquelyn Grant

Jacquelyn Grant is known for her critical womanist approach to the Christological question, an issue not fully explored in Black Theology. Her book, *White Woman's Christ, Black Woman's Jesus*,[49] gives an affirmative but nuanced response to the continually raised question of white feminist theologians, "Can a male be the saviour of women?" The point of departure for her theological endeavor goes beyond the feminist critique of historical and contemporary male theology which she sees as inadequate for its failure to critique its own limited foundation in the Euro-American world-view and to raise "...racism/sexism/classism, as a conglomerate representation of oppression [as] the most adequate point of departure for doing the kind of wholistic theology and Christology which...feminist theologians advocate."[50]

Black women representing an embodiment of this triply oppressive reality possess the potential for a wholistic analysis that can provide for the development of wholistic theological and Christological construction(s) which are wholly rather than partially liberating.[51]

Womanist theology begins, not with an emphasis on the liberation of women alone, but on the liberation of an entire community with the women's struggle seen as a focal point encompassing all other struggles along the lines of race, gender, and class. Thus, Grant contextualizes her exploration of the meaning of Jesus Christ in the context of women, particularly Black women who, however, are themselves grounded in and emerge from a particular community, the African American community in the United States.

She critically attacks feminist theology for two reasons: it is *white* and it is *racist*, noting that the experience upon which it is based is "almost exclusively" that of white women which differs in critical ways (as previously discussed) from the experience of Black and other women of color.[52] The historical context of Black and white women's lives is separated, she notes, by the gulf created by slavery and segregation.

What is apparent in this historical context is how Black women's experience involves a convergence of racism, sexism and classism. Within the limited arena of domestic labor, the sexist assumption that women's place is [only] in the home is reconfirmed, as well as the classist practice of paying those who do 'menial' jobs little or nothing, and the assumption that such work is more appropriately done by those of the servant class. These patterns are compounded by the racist assumption that white women need protection from actual work and, therefore, should function in a supervisory capacity.[53]

Thus, it is the Black woman's experience, which goes beyond these limitations/restrictions, that serves as the context from which Grant's Christology emerges. Recognizing that, for Black women, the Bible is considered "a major source for religious validation in their lives," she presents a twofold source for their understanding of God: first, that of God's direct revelation to them as Black women, and, second, God's revelation as witnessed in the Bible and as received in the context of their lived-out experience, God revealed as Creator, Sustainer of life, Comforter, and Liberator.[54]

Jesus, therefore, is seen as the "divine co-sufferer, who empowers [Blacks] in situations of oppression."[55] He is the central frame of reference. Yet she also makes the point (in chapter four of her work) that there is, for African Americans, no difference made between the persons of the Trinity. Quoting Harold Carter: "All of these proper names for God (as Father, Son, Holy Spirit) were used interchangeably in prayer language.... Jesus was the one who speaks the world into creation. He was the power behind the Church."[56]

Black women, for Grant, because of their triple oppression, are the "particular within the particular," the oppressed of the oppressed.[57]

> To speak of Black women's tri-dimensional reality, therefore, is not to speak of Black women exclusively, for there is an implied universality which connects them with others.[58]

This connection can be found, in terms of racial oppression, with Black men and other people of color, in terms of gender oppression, with white women and other women of color, and, in terms of class, with both Blacks and whites at the bottom of the economic scale in American society.

For us the Resurrection signified that there is more to life than the cross for Jesus Christ, for Black women it signifies that their tri-dimensional oppressive existence is not the end, but it merely represents the context in which a particular people struggle to experience hope and liberation.[59]

Jesus Christ, therefore, is seen as identifying with the "least among us," affirming their basic humanity and inspiring "active hope in [their] struggle for [a] resurrected, liberated existence."[60]

Grant presents several challenges for the further development of a womanist Christology. She calls upon Black women to "investigate the relationship between the oppression of women and theological symbolism," recognizing the inadequacy of some traditional symbols today. As she notes, "The Christ understood as the stranger, the outcast, the hungry, the weak, the poor, makes the traditional male Christ (both Black and white) less significant."[61] This challenge raises an ontological issue: If Christ is the Savior of all, not just men, then is not all of Christ's humanity significant, that is, the wholeness of Christ. That significance lies not in his maleness but in his humanness. "For [Jarena] Lee, this meant women could preach; for Sojourner [Truth], it meant that women could possibly save the world; for me [Grant], it means today, this Christ, found in the experiences of Black women, is a Black woman."[62]

Second, she sees the need for womanist theologians to explore, in greater depth, the question of Christ's meaning in a society in which class distinctions are increasing. A race/gender analysis leads to the realization "that Blacks and women should share in the leadership of the church [but the present] style virtually insures the continuation of a privileged class."[63] Thus, a "serious analysis which addresses the structural nature of poverty" is necessary.

Lastly, Grant challenges womanist theologians to develop a constructive Christology, one which is liberating for both the Black women's community and the larger Black community, recognizing that "A Christology which negates Black male humanity is still destructive to the Black community."[64]

The "very embodiment" of these challenges represent, as she notes, a challenge to white women which is ongoing. "This embodiment [of racism, sexism and classism] says to white women that a wholistic analysis is a minimal requirement for a wholistic theology. The task of Black women, then, is constructive."[65]

Kelly Brown Douglas

In a more recent work, *The Black Christ*,[66] Kelly Brown Douglas extends the challenge of a womanist perspective on Christ even further, providing an important introduction to the historical and religious significance of the Black Christ for African Americans. Tracing the Black understanding of Jesus Christ from the time of slavery to the present day, she sees that understanding as being centered on Christ's liberating role as "a stand against White racism and for Black freedom" which has "empowered Black Christians and Black churches to be prophetic in relation to issues of race in America."[67] At the same time, she critiques the apparent inability of that same Church of liberation "to empower and nurture more than one half of its own constituency, Black women."[68]

The first part of this work explores the meaning of the Black Christ historically while the second part is an analysis of the "potential and limitations" of the Black

Christ. It is in the last chapter, "A Womanist Approach to the Black Christ," that Douglas raises and answers the question: "Does the Black Christ adequately point to Christ's significance and presence within the contemporary Black community?"

She first approaches this question from a socio-political analysis of wholeness which "will confront racism, sexism, classism, and heterosexism not only as they impinge upon the Black community, but also as they are nurtured within that community,"[69] revealing how both the Black community and Black institutions contribute to and perpetuate Black oppression.

Douglas then moves to a religio-cultural analysis which "lifts up" aspects of Black life that sustain and nurture while denying those which retard survival and liberation.

> A religio-cultural analysis recognizes that not everything 'Black' necessarily benefits the Black community…. What was once labeled "Black consciousness" can now be seen in the call for Afrocentrism. The Afrocentric concern attempts to trace the roots, especially African roots, of African American culture in an effort to nurture self-esteem and cultural pride in African Americans. A religio-cultural analysis would challenge those involved with the Afrocentric project to critically evaluate what they unearth, to recognize that just because something is African or Black does not signify that it has value for Black people as they move toward wholeness.[70]

In short, for her "a religio-cultural analysis attempts to highlight that which has allowed Black women to transcend the negative, dehumanizing images that society has maintained of them," assuming the presence of a "spirituality of resistance" which Black women have nurtured and passed on.[71]

There is a difference between the Christologies of
Grant and Brown, however. While both acknowledge the
importance of both the biblical and Black women's
witness to Christ and, in so doing, disavow the centrality
of Jesus' maleness as a determining factor for understanding his meaning, Grant presents, as noted above, a
tridimensional analysis encompassing race, gender, and
class while Douglas' analysis is both multidimensional
and bifocal, confronting, as she herself states, "all that
oppresses the Black community as it impinges upon the
community or is harbored within." Thus, "Christ is a
sustainer, liberator, and prophet in the face of such evil
as racism, sexism, classism, and heterosexism."[72]

Douglas also believes that Grant's image of Christ as a
Black woman, when found in Black women's experience,
does not allow for the "possibility of Christ's being seen
in the faces of black men who also struggle for Black
women's and men's lives and wholeness." However, this
distinction is not fully developed, for she also, in the end,
acknowledges, as Grant did, that Christ is a Black
woman, "...when Black women are acting to establish
life and wholeness for the Black community."[73] The two
stances are not that different.

Conclusion

Womanist theology serves as a critical challenge to the
way theology has been taught and practiced historically.
Within its ranks are women from every walk of life, lay,
ordained and religious, with perspectives that overlap
but also differ. It is not, nor can it or any theology be, a
monolithic one, yet it attempts to present the state of
Black America today and to raise questions that are in
sync with the concerns of men and women who have been

seen as marginal and who have been silenced by the historical articulators of theological wisdom. They bring a much needed voice that is being listened to and acted upon throughout the Christian churches, one which is changing not only our image of Church and theology, but our very way of being Church and doing theology.

Black Catholic women have also begun to develop a womanist hermeneutic in their efforts to theologize from their experience as Black, Catholic, and female. Their efforts are an important part of the development, as well, of a Black Catholic Theology, as will be discussed in Chapter Eight.

Notes

1. The reasons for the "invisibility" of Black Catholics is discussed in Chapter Eight.

2. Evelyn Brooks Higginbotham, in *Righteous Discontent: The Women's Movement in the Black Baptist Church, 1880-1920* (Cambridge, Ma.: Harvard University Press, 1993), presents, in depth, both the challenge of Black women and the challenges to them in the Baptist Church. Recent research on and recovery of the "lost" diaries and autobiographies of Black women preachers, eldresses, exhorters and evangelists reveals for us today the profound involvement and influence of Black women in the Black Church and community. See Henry Louis Gates, ed., *Spiritual Narratives: M.W. Stewart, J. Lee, J.A.J. Foote, V.W. Broughton* and *Amanda Smith, An Autobiography: The Story of the Lord's Dealings with Mrs A. Smith, the Colored Evangelist*, both in The Schomburg Library of Nineteenth Century Writers (N.Y.: Oxford University Press, 1988) as well as *Gifts of Power: The Writings of Rebecca Jackson, Black Visionary, Shaker Eldress* (Amherst: University of Massachusetts Press, 1981), and Ella Mitchell, *Those Preaching Women*, among others.

3. There are two Black female Bishops in the United States; Leontine T.C. Kelly is the first Black woman to be installed as a Bishop of a major religious denomination, the United Methodist Church in 1984. Barbara Harris is the first woman as well as the first Black woman to be named a Bishop in the Episcopal Church (1989).

4. See Frances Beale, "Double Jeopardy: To Be Black and Female," and Theressa Hoover, "Black Women and the Churches: Triple Jeopardy" in Cone and Wilmore, *Black Theology*, Vol. I, pp. 284-292 and 293-303.

5. (New York: Harper and Row, 1990), originally published, 1937.

6. Ibid., p. 29.

6a. See Elisabeth Schüssler Fiorenza, Discipleship of Equals: A Critical Feminist Ekklesia-logy of Liberation (New York: Crossroad, 1993), for discussion of the role of the "White Lady."

7. "Experiences of the Race Problem. By a Southern White Woman," *Independent*, 56 (17 March 1904) as cited in Higginbotham, *Righteous Discontent*.

8. See Susan Brooks Thislethwaite, *Sex, Race and God: Christian Feminism in Black and White* (New York: Crossroad, 1989).

9. Ibid., p. 33.

10. bell hooks, *Ain't I A Woman?: Black Women and Feminism* (Boston: South End Press, 1981), p. 28.

11. Hurston, *Their Eyes*, pp. 32-35.

12. See Gloria I. Joseph and Jill Lewis, *Common Differences: Conflicts in Black and White Feminist Perspectives* (Boston: South End Press, 1981) for a fuller discussion on this point as well as the many writings of bell hooks on feminism.

13. bell hooks, *Feminist Theory: From Margin to Center* (Boston, Ma.: South End Press, 1984), p. 23.

14. Patricia Hill Collins, *Black Feminist Thought: Knowledge, Consciousness, and the Politics of Empowerment* (New York: Routledge, 1991, vol. 2, *Perspectives on Gender*), pp. xii-xiii.

15. Ibid.

16. *In Search of Our Mothers' Gardens: Womanist Prose* (New York: Harcourt Brace Jovanovich, 1983), p. xi. Walker's definition, although inclusive of the Spirit, is not a theological one. Black women theologians have adopted the term as a form of self-definition based on Walker's and, as will be seen, are continuing to expand on it from their particular contexts and experiences as Black Christian women.

17. Ibid.

18. *Sisters in the Wilderness* (Maryknoll, NY: Orbis, 1993).

19. *White Woman's Christ, Black Woman's Jesus* (Atlanta, Ga.: Scholars Press, 1989).

20. *Black Womanist Ethics* (Scholars Press, 1988); an interesting interview of Dr. Cannon and her influence is presented by Sara Lawrence-Lightfoot, ed., *I've Known Rivers: Lives of Loss and Liberation* (Reading, Ma.: Addison-Wesley Publishing Co., 1994).

21. Ed., *A Troubling in My Soul: Womanist Perspectives on Evil and Suffering* (Maryknoll, N.Y.: Orbis Books, 1994), author of *Womanist Justice, Womanist Hope* (Atlanta, Ga.: Scholars Press, 1994) and *In a Blaze of Glory: Womanist Spirituality as Social Witness* (Nashville: Abingdon Press, 1995).

22. *Just a Sister Away: A Womanist Vision of Women's Relationships in the Bible* (San Diego: LuraMedia, 1988).

23. *Living the Intersection*, previously cited.

24. *The Black Christ* (Maryknoll, N.Y.: Orbis Books, 1994).

25. *Lifting As We Climb: A Womanist Ethic of Care* (forthcoming, Abingdon Press), and with James Newton Poling, *Balm for Gilead: Pastoral Advocacy for African American Families Experiencing Abuse* (Nashville: Abingdon Press, 1995).

26. *Hagar's Daughters: Womanist Ways of Being in the World* (Mahwah, N.J.: Paulist Press, 1994) and *Trouble Don't Last Always: Soul Prayers* (Collegeville, Mn: The Liturgical Press, 1995).

27. Hooks, *Feminist Theory*, p. 15.

28. Collins, *Black Feminist Thought*, see especially ch. 11, "The Matrix of Domination," pp. 225ff.

29. Cannon, *Black Womanist Ethics*, p. 12.

30. Ibid., p. 11.

31. Ibid., p. 8.

32. Ibid.

33. Ibid., p. 12.

34. Ibid., pp. 3-4.

35. Ibid.

36. Ibid., p. 6; also see footnote 4.

37. See, for example, Higginbotham, *Righteous Discontent*; Mary Helen Washington, *Invented Lives: Narratives of Black Women, 1860-1960* (Garden City, NY: Doubleday, 1978); Henry Louis Gates, ed. *Spiritual Narratives*; Alice Walker, *In Search of...*; Paula Giddings, *When and Where I Enter: The Impact of Black Women on Race and Sex in America* (New York: William Morrow, 1984); Gerda Lerner, ed. *Black Women in White America: A Documentary History* (New York: Vintage, 1973); and, most recent, Darlene Clark Hine, ed. *Black Women in*

America: An Historical Encyclopedia (Brooklyn: Carlson Publishing, 1993).

38. *Black Womanist Ethics*, p. 7.

39. in *Christianity and Crisis* (March 2, 1987), pp. 66-67; she has expanded on this in her work, *Sisters in the Wilderness: Womanist Theology* (Maryknoll, NY: Orbis, 1993). All page citations are from the article as published in Mar Peter-Raoul et al., ed., *Yearning To Breath Free: Liberation Theologies in the U.S.* (Maryknoll, N.Y.: Orbis Books, 1990), pp. 62-68.

40. Ibid., p. 66.

41. Ibid., p. 67.

42. Ibid.

43. Ibid.

44. Ibid., p. 68.

45. *Sisters*, pp. 60-61.

46. Ibid., pp. 161-167.

47. Ibid.

48. See works previously cited and *Black Theology: A Documentary History, Volume II: 1980-1992* (Maryknoll, NY: Orbis, 1993), Part IV: Womanist Theology, which presents writings by Delores Williams, Jacquelyn Grant, Kelly Brown-Douglass, Katie Cannon, Toinette Eugene, Cheryl Townsend Gilkes, Diana L. Hayes, Cheryl Saunders and Renee Hill. An important accompaniment to Williams' critique of surrogacy is Townes, ed., *A Troubling in My Soul*, which explores the persistent questions of evil and suffering from the perspective of a number of womanist theologians.

49. (Atlanta: Scholars Press, 1989).

50. Ibid. p. 2.

51. Ibid.

52. Ibid., p. 195.

53. Ibid., p. 198.

54. Ibid., p. 211.

55. Ibid., p. 212.

56. Carter, *The Prayer Tradition*, p. 50.

57. *White Woman's Christ*, p. 216.

58. Ibid., p. 217.

59. Ibid.

60. Ibid., p. 218.

61. Ibid., p. 219.

62. Ibid., p. 220.

63. Ibid., p. 221.

64. Ibid.

65. Ibid., pp. 221-222.

66. (Maryknoll, New York: Orbis Books, 1994).

67. Ibid., p. 3.

68. Ibid., p. 4.

69. Ibid., p. 99.

70. Ibid., pp. 104-105.

71. Ibid., p. 105.

72. Ibid., p. 109.

73. Ibid., p. 110.

8

The Development
of a Black
Catholic Theology

The other voice historically absent from Black Liberation Theology has been that of Black Catholics who, in the past three decades, have begun to engage in God-talk from within the context of their marginalized status both in the Roman Catholic Church and, too often, in the Black community itself.

In the writings of many Black theologians, references to Black Catholics, to the Roman Catholic Church in the United States, its history and traditions, and to the efforts toward self-expression of Black Catholics in the nineteenth and twentieth centuries, are few and far between. Black Catholics have been invisible both to those inside and outside of the Roman Catholic Church.[1] Today, Black Catholics number approximately three million in the United States, a minority within that Church, perhaps, but a significant number in terms of Black Christians and an increasingly important voice in a nation and world in which people of color are becoming, if they are not already, the majority. The fastest growing Church in the Catholic communion is that of Africa which recently held its first continent-wide synod to address the issues and concerns of African Catholics.[2]

The absence of the voice of Black Catholics from the dialogue is a serious but in many ways understandable one. As we have seen, Black Liberation Theology is, like other liberation theologies, a contextual theology. As those who first articulated this theology in a systematic form did so from their own contextual experience, one mainly Protestant in nature, and engaged in dialogue within the ranks of the historically Black Churches, it is natural to assume that their evolving theology would be one Protestant in its perspective.[3]

At the same time, as noted in Chapter Two, ordination to the priesthood for Black men, the accepted path to leadership in the Roman Catholic Church, was not encouraged in the United States until the present century, while religious vocations, for men and women, were also actively discouraged.[4] Thus, until the reforms of the Synod of Vatican II in the Roman Catholic Church (which took place between 1962 and 1965 and dramatically shifted the Church's perspective on lay involvement) and the Civil Rights and ensuing movements leading up to the emergence of Black Liberation Theology in the Protestant Church, the involvement of Black Catholic scholars has been limited in number and restricted in voice. They are still few in number today, but that number is growing as more Black Catholics enter programs of graduate theological study. They are joined with and supported by a very strong and active laity involved in the Black Catholic Congress movement with roots dating back to the latter part of the nineteenth century.[5]

As Black Catholic men and women have begun to explore their richly diverse history and to speak out of their own unique contexts, they are challenging and reformulating our understanding of Black Theology. In so doing, they make the assertion that to be Black and Catholic is not paradoxical, contradictory or contrary to the Black Liberation Movement but is simply one of the many flowing streams which make up the river of the Black experience in the United States. Their voices and experience bear witness to a long hidden and often neglected Black experience and tradition which dates back to the early Church in Africa itself[6] and which has been nurtured and sustained under both slavery and freedom in the United States.[7]

The Black Presence in the Early Church

Despite changing demographics which reveal a Catholic Church increasingly made up of people of color, the Church's public image is not Black or multi-hued, it is white and European, an image which denies the history of the Church's origins in the Middle East and Africa.

Only in recent years, as Black and other scholars have begun to question the historical assumption that Christianity is a European faith in origins and tradition, has a recovery process begun that is critically revealing of those origins. Few Christians, regardless of race, ethnicity or denomination, have been fully aware, until recently, of the rich diversity of the Christian Church at its birth or of its syncretic nature, merging traditions and rituals from many sources in its evolution. In discussing the Church Fathers, their African back-grounds are usually passed over or restricted to North Africa, a region which has historically been seen as somehow separate and apart from "Black" Africa. Rarely is mention made of the African ancestry of three Popes (Militiades, Victor, and Gelasius), of the many African martyrs and saints, such as Felicity and Perpetua whose names are daily recited in the Eucharistic Prayer of the Roman Rite, or of the origins of the monastic movement in the African desert, led by St. Moses the Black who was martyred in 410 A.D.[8]

The first known convert to Christianity was Nubian, the Ethiopian eunuch, as set forth in the Acts of the Apostles (Acts 8:26-40). Christianity flourished and was sustained in Ethiopia, Egypt, and much of Nubian (Black) Africa long before it was transformed into a European faith.

> Long before Christianity arrived in the Scandinavian countries, at least a century before St. Patrick evangelized Ireland, and over two centuries before St. Augustine would arrive in Canterbury, and almost seven centuries before the conversion of the Poles and the establishment of the kingdom of Poland, this mountainous black kingdom (Ethiopia) was a Catholic nation with its own liturgy, its own spectacular religious art, its own monastic tradition, its saints and its own spirituality.[9]

The true history of the Black presence in the Church is only today beginning to emerge.

The Catholic Church was Greek, Roman and Jewish in its origins but also African, and continues to be so to the present day. The problem which haunts the Church today, after its long European captivity, arises from its failure or inability to fully and freely immerse itself into the lives, traditions, and cultures of a people historically seen as "less than" human, without cultures or traditions worthy of notice.

This is rapidly changing, however. Black Catholics are today engaged in a process of self-redefinition, socially, historically, liturgically and theologically, supported by the Holy Father.

[Y]our black cultural heritage enriches the church and makes her witness of universality more complete. In a real way the church needs you just as you need the church, for you are a part of the church and the church is part of you.[10]

Looking at a Church in which they have been a part for over four hundred years, they see an institution which has tolerated their presence but not encouraged it; an institution which has required that they give up much of what was naturally and legitimately theirs in order to become a part of an often sterile and oppressive system in which many have never felt fully at home. Yet, they have persevered.

They are speaking out at every level of the Church on issues of concern, particularly their persistent and faith-filled presence in a Church which has historically denied their full participation and leadership.

Black Catholics, like all Christians before them, are seeking to understand their relationship with God and God's relationship with them, in language of their own creation. They are raising questions theological in nature which challenge themselves and the Church: Who is God for us as Catholics? What does it mean to witness to Christ as a Black Catholic? What is significant about our understanding of Mary, the Mother of God, of Jesus, the Son of God, and of God, the Creator and the Holy Spirit, and how are they a part of our lives? How do we express these understandings in ways that are expressive of our heritage as people of African roots yet with American branches?

They are engaged in expanding the dialogue now taking place in Black Theology, emphasizing the heritage which they share as people of African descent with their fellow Blacks in other Churches, but doing so from a tradition which, as Catholics, is and should be different, as befitting their own unique contextual situation.[11]

Black Catholics are aware of the pitfalls in their path, especially of the dangers, as revealed by those who have come before them, such as Cone and others, of relying too heavily on the efforts of Euro-Catholic scholars such as Karl Rahner, Johann Baptist Metz and others or even of those who are at work in similar fields of Liberation Theology such as Gustavo Gutierrez, Juan Luis Segundo et al.[12] Their contexts are different and cannot be universalized to fit the faith life and experience of others. Although recognizing that they share traditions as Catholics, members of a universal Church, Black Catholics acknowledge as well the differences in their historical experience and their present day existence and realize the necessity to free themselves to critique both the Catholic Church and other Catholic theologians, if and when necessary, in order to fully and freely express their own vision of Catholicism. They seek to look at the Church through Black eyes, recognizing its shortcomings as revealed in the long, sordid history of racism, sexism, and classism in the Church but also its strengths which have enabled and encouraged them to remain, albeit too long silent, and to continue proclaiming the life, death and resurrection of Jesus Christ with Black voices.

The United States Bishops have acknowledged the Church's deformation of the Gospel's mandate to love one another, noting that "Racism is an evil which endures in our society and in our church."[13] Much of what the pastoral letter on racism said in 1979 sadly still holds true today:

> Today the sense of urgency has yielded to an apparent acceptance of the status quo. The climate of crisis engendered by demonstrations, protests, and confronta-

tion has given way to a mood of indifference; and other issues occupy our attention.[14]

In many ways, the situation for Blacks in the Catholic Church in the United States has not changed. Despite papal and other documents which have allegedly opened doors to new forms of expression in the Church and new ways of "being" Church together across racial, class, and gender lines, in actuality the unique contribution of a people, forged in slavery and oppression, yet full of hope and love, is still often ignored or condemned as inappropriate.

Paul VI stated in his epistle, "To the Heart of Africa":

> The language and mode of manifesting the one faith may be manifold. Hence, it may be original, suited to the tongue, the style, the characteristics, the genius and the culture of one who professes this one faith. From this point of view, a certain pluralism is not only legitimate, but desirable.
>
> An adaptation of the Christian life and the fields of pastoral, ritual, didactic and spiritual activities is not only possible, it is favored by the church. The liturgical renewal is a living example of this. And, in this sense, you may and you must have an African Christianity. Indeed, you possess human values and forms of culture which can rise up to perfection, such as to find in Christianity a true, superior fullness and prove to be capable of a richness of expression all of its own and genuinely African.[15]

The Catholic Church is today being challenged by Black Catholics (and other heretofore marginalized groups) to live up to this mandate and truly inculturate itself within the rich heritage of blackness which persists within the Church, enabling a give and take which can be reviving and renewing for both the Church and all of its people.

As Father Clarence Rivers noted almost three decades ago:

> The Catholic church will remain religiously ineffective in the black community unless it can effectively syncretize African culture with Catholic worship, just as the black Protestant church two centuries ago syncretized African culture and Biblical religion.[16]

Black people have remained in the Catholic Church against all odds. That they have done so is due to their perseverance and their faith in the truth of the Gospel more than the encouragement of the Church itself:

> Black presence in the predominantly white Christian church is also an affirmation that Christian faith, rooted firmly in an uncompromised Gospel, speaks with clarity and directness to the heart of the black experience— namely the individual as well as collective quest for recognition of human dignity and personal worth. It is further a challenge.[17]

Black Catholics are merging their own rich tradition with the Roman Catholic tradition and its colorful ritual and sacramentality. They are creating new forms of worship, new ways of being Church which honor and uphold the values of both traditions. In so doing, they are once again transforming Christianity, as their slave forebears did, centuries ago, and as Blacks have continued to do throughout their existence in the Christian Church. They are engaged in the work of inculturation, a critical aspect of the continued evolution of Christianity in keeping with the "signs of the times":

> [Inculturation means]...the incarnation of Christian life and of the Christian message in a particular cultural context, in such a way that this experience not only finds

expression through elements proper to the culture in question, but becomes a principle that animates, directs and unifies the culture, transforming and remaking it so as to bring about a "new creation."[18]

They are doing this, often not only against opposition from their pastors and Church, but from other Black Catholics who have been, for too long, molded by values other than their own.

For they realize that they must also look at their own failings and critique them with an eye toward strengthening their Black self-identity and self-expression. They must respond to the charges of "one-up-manship," of self-hatred and denial of their rich history and culture in order to be accepted in a Church which encouraged them to deny their past and adapt to a present exclusive of their rich and diverse gifts.

Black Catholicism: The Source of a Black Catholic Theology

What is distinctive about Black Catholicism? To be Catholic is to be aware of the two foundations upon which the Church and its teachings stand: Scripture and tradition. Yet one must recognize and assert that tradition, not as of one unchangeable heritage but as the result of the mingled strands of traditions of all of those who name themselves Catholic and their lived experience of their faith as it is revealed to them and lived out. As Christianity was once inculturated into the Jewish, African, Greek, Roman and eventually European cultures, the peoples of Africa, Asia, and Latin America and their descendants in the United States are calling for true inculturation to take place within their cultures as well.[19] This calls for the recognition of the existence and

validity of those cultures as bearers of and fertile soil for
Christianity as well as for cultural retrieval and revival
by the bearers of those cultures, many of whom have
been alienated from them.

> Through Christ, the non-repeatable historical event
> becomes actual, and Christ continues to be actively
> present in the world. The extent of the Church's incarna-
> tion in various roles and cultures will be the extent of
> Christ's universality. The Incarnation is a historical
> event, but its universality lives on wherever the Church
> assumes the social and cultural conditions of the people
> among whom she dwells.... The Church must incarnate
> herself in every race, as Christ has incarnated himself in
> the Jewish race.[20]

Over the centuries of the Black presence in this country and in the Catholic Church, Black Catholics have, in
many ways, been co-opted and corrupted into supporting
the status quo, in forsaking their own unique identities
in their quest to be seen as truly Catholic. This is
not unique to only Catholics. Today, however, African
American Catholics are speaking out on what it means
to them to be "truly Black and authentically Catholic" in
a holistic, life-affirming and community-building way.
They are articulating that meaning for themselves and
others in the development of a theology and spirituality
which arises out of the context of their own lived
experience in the United States.

> Today we as an African American people are engaged in
> the development of a theology that speaks truly to us and
> expresses who we are and whose we are for the enlight-
> enment of the entire church.
> We are African Americans. We are a people with roots
> deeply sunk in the history and culture of our African
> homeland yet also a people with a long and proud history

in these United States. Both strands of our heritage are important in defining who we are; neither can be denied without denying an important part of our very selves.

Thus to say that we are African Americans is to say a lot. That understanding of "who we are and whose we are" impacts upon our theologizing. It "colors," quite simply, our concept of God, our faith in Jesus Christ, our existence in the Holy Spirit, our total understanding of what it means to be truly black and authentically Catholic. Thus, our reflections are not abstract or objective, they are particular....

Our way of theologizing stems from our understanding of and faith in a God who "makes a way out of no way," a God who can be "leaned on" in times of trial and tribulation; a God who is an active, interested and loving participant in our history—and has been from the very beginning of our sojourn in this country and long before.[21]

The spirituality of Black Catholics, as with all Black Christians, is biblically-centered. Sacred Scripture is neither wholly rejected nor is it accepted uncritically. Their experience in slavery taught them to read the Bible with Black eyes and to proclaim the Word of God with Black voices and understanding. Unmoved by the efforts of masters to implant a biased and distorted Christianity, Black Christians, as previously noted, re-Christianized Christianity, opening it up to its fullest understanding as a religion of liberation proclaiming a God who created free men and women in God's own image and who gave them a Liberator in Christ Jesus, the Son of God.

The Black Catholic understanding of God and Christ is therefore also "colored," if you will, by that liberationist understanding. God and Jesus are not problematical; they are both immanent and transcendent in our lives. The immanent God loves us and nurtures us like a parent bending low over a child, yet as transcendent God is free to judge those who oppress us and to call us forth into freedom. Jesus as immanent humanity is brother, sister, and friend; he is in all ways one with us, walking and talking with us, sharing our journey and carrying our burdens, and suffering the pain of our oppression and rejection, yet, as transcendent Son of God, he will come forth in glory to lead us to the Promised Land. And we rejoice in the Holy Spirit, that balm of Gilead sent to heal our sin-sick souls, to abide within us and to strengthen us on our journey while giving us the courage to fight back against our oppressors and to "keep on keepin' on."

It is in Catholicism that the transplanted Africans found a home "of sorts" which nurtured their traditional religiosity. The saints and sacramentals, feast and fast days, processions and rituals were strikingly familiar to a people comfortable with the concept of a High God, of intercessions and special rites and rituals in their life of worship. At the same time, they were denied their more fervent expressions of faith and the music which helped them draw closer to God.[22]

Yet they remained in the Church, despite neglect and often active opposition, often stealing away to be with other Black Christians, as in the "hush arbor" days of slavery to remain in touch with their culture and to be nurtured and sustained. Yet they remained faithful. They are now reaffirming that long-lost heritage, bringing it to the altar of Christ to share with all of the People of God. They are systematizing their faith and beginning to articulate it in ways that are healing and holy, yet also challenging, for all.

African Americans bring to the Catholic Church a long and rich tradition, one in part shared since the Church's earliest beginnings, as revealed in the baptism of the Ethiopian eunuch, yet, in other ways, one uniquely new, the result of the creation of a new people, both African and American. They bring a tradition that can arguably be seen as "subversive," one which is paradoxical, turning all of accepted reality upside down to present a new reality, that of the last being called forth to be revealed as the bearers of a vital, healing vision of Christ crucified from their experience of both racial and religious persecution. They reflect the memory of a Church that has preached equality while practicing discrimination and segregation, a Church that has preached a God of love while practicing racial hatred and division.[23]

Yet they also bring a healing and holy sacramentality, an extension of the "welcome table" to all of God's people as evidenced in their Gospel liturgies which invite and create new communities of Catholics from all walks of life, of all colors and classes, thus bringing about a new Church which is truly representative of the entire people of God in its catholicity.

Black Catholics also speak of Mary, the Mother of God, in new and challenging ways, rejecting the symbol of passivity for the courageous and outrageous authority of a young unwed mother who had the faith in herself and in her God to break through the limitations her society placed upon her to say a powerful and prophetic "yes" to God, standing alone yet empowered. Hers was not a "yes" to being used merely as a passive, empty vessel but a "yes" to empowerment, challenging the status quo by her ability to overcome those who doubted and denied her to nurture and bring forth her son as a woman of faith and conviction.

As descendants of Mother Africa and representative of the far-flung African diaspora, Black Catholics also recognize their strength in communion with Black Catholics around the world, the fastest growing body in the universal Church and one coming into its own as a people of faith, in communion with the Church in Rome, but representative of new voices, new expressions, new styles of worship, new language about God which feeds the needs of millions, not just in the United States, but throughout the world.

The State of Black Catholic Scholarship

Black scholars are still few in number with only five holding doctorates in systematic theology,[24] yet they are beginning to explore and set forth the parameters of a Black Catholic Theology in articles and longer works in progress. Working in conjunction with the growing number of Black Catholic scholars from various religious and interdisciplinary fields, they are engaged in the process of contextualizing Black Theology in and through the Black Catholic experience.

Fr. Cyprian Davis, a Church historian, has been in the forefront of this effort for the past twenty years, presenting lectures and papers which "retrieve, contextualize, and interpret both Black Catholic models of sanctity and African American Catholic spiritual traditions of communal Bible study and prayer."[25] His most significant contribution has been in lifting the veil of ignorance concerning the history, past and present, of peoples of African descent in the Roman Catholic Church and Christianity from its earliest beginnings.

Other Black Catholic scholars are also engaged in exploring new territory with regard to Black Catholics and the Church and American society. Edward Braxton has written extensively and critically on Black Protestant Theology and Black Catholic theological and pastoral endeavors, including the VIth National Black Catholic Congress (1987).[26]

Shawn Copeland's work has been particularly in the area of methodology. Currently she is working on a methodological approach to a Black Catholic Political Theology and a reformulation of "political theology in the American context with specific attention to issues of race, gender, and class." She also was the Program Director for the National Black Theology Project and, as a result, has been actively engaged in dialogue with Black Protestants as well as theologians of all backgrounds for some time.

Jamie Phelps has been active in exploring the psychosocial theme of Black self-concept. Her doctoral work was done in ecclesiology and she has written widely in the areas of Church, spirituality, Christology, missiology and personhood from a Black perspective. As a member of EATWOT, the Ecumenical Association of Third World Theologians, she has been engaged in dialogue with theologians from Africa, Asia, and Latin America as well as within the United States. Phelps, Copeland, and Braxton were participants in the first two Black Catholic Theological Symposiums, and the latter two continue to actively participate in it.

Albert Raboteau, author of the previously cited *Slave Religion*, has been instrumental in providing an understanding of the Black religious experience during the period of slavery and is one of the first to present the Black Catholic experience as an important aspect. He also presents an argument for the retention of aspects of African culture during and after slavery.

Toinette Eugene, with a doctorate in religion and society, has been involved in the development of a Black Catholic theology of catechesis as well as the moral and ethical parameters of Black Catholic catechesis. She writes extensively in the area of catechesis, the Black family, and womanist theology.

My own work has focused on the development of a contextual theology for the United States, representative of the full diversity of the people of this land but grounded specifically in the faith of those historically marginalized, as well as the parameters for a Black Catholic Theology of Liberation. In addition, I have written on issues of liturgical inculturation, pastoral ministry, the Black Family and Black spirituality.

Fr. Bryan Massengale, a moral theologian, has been working in the area of racism and the social teachings of the Catholic Church, while Fr. Philip Linden, who is in the process of completing his doctorate in systematic theology, is also working on the issue of racism and the Catholic Church. Fr. Thaddeus Posey, one of the original members of the Symposium and Director for several years of The Institute for Black Catholic Studies at Xavier University, recently completed his dissertation in Church History on the Oblate Sisters of Providence, the oldest Black religious order in the United States.

As can be seen, the numbers, however, are still very few. The recently reconstituted Black Catholic Theological Symposium is one approach that Black Catholics are taking to bring together Black Catholic scholars from various disciplines, including theology, in order to dialogue with and be in support of each other in their various fields while exploring the parameters for a Black Catholic Theology in all of its hoped-for richness and diversity. Most are involved with the Master of Theology in Black Catholic Studies program at Xavier and in other programs such as the Augustus Tolton program at Chicago Theological Union which seek to identify, encourage and foster more Black Catholic scholars in the fields of theology and religious studies.

Black Catholic theology is still in its formative stages as Black Catholics gather in their parishes, revivals, diocesan meetings and, most importantly, nationwide events such as the National Black Congresses,[27] to engage in "God-talk" from their own context and perspective. As Protestant Blacks did, Black Catholics are raising questions of critical significance for themselves as a people who are both Black and Catholic: Who is God for us? What does it mean to witness to Christ as a Catholic who is Black? Is there a Black understanding of the Church, of Scripture, of Mary, the Mother of Jesus and, if so, how do we articulate that understanding? Their response to the latter is a resounding yes as they go about the work of articulating that understanding.[28]

They seek what is distinctive about Black Catholicism, a sharing of African roots with their Black Protestant brothers and sisters[29] as expressed in their celebration of Christ in song and word but also an appreciation of the importance of both Scripture and tradition intertwined with an emphasis on a sacramentality which is Catholic in its foundation but Black in its expression.[30] Black Catholics in the United States, in sharing the tradition of the Church from its earliest beginnings, bring a critique of that tradition, serving as a "subversive memory" within the Church itself which calls it to live up to its proclamation of Scriptures which reveal God's consistent option for the poor and the oppressed but which have been too often submerged by a praxis which ignored the plight of those same poor and oppressed.

Black Catholic Womanist Theology

One particularly fruitful avenue for bringing a new and Catholic perspective to Black Liberation Theology is through the context of Black Catholic women who can be seen, as all women can, as the "bearers of culture,"[31] those who birth a people and a world into being. It is here that womanist theology and Black Theology converge, in the voices of women who have been oppressed because of their race, their gender and their faith.

When we speak of oppression in the Roman Catholic Church, we cannot look simply at the experiences of white women nor only at the suffering of Black men. Neither is, nor can be, truly reflective of what it means to be Black, Catholic and female in the Catholic Church today.[32]

It is, perhaps, in their reinterpretation of the role and presence of Mary, the Mother of God, that Black Catholic women can make the most significant contribution. Too often seen as a docile, submissive woman, Black Catholic womanists, instead, see a young woman sure of her God and of her role in God's salvific plan. She is a woman who, in her song (Lk 1:46–55), proclaims her allegiance with God and with her brothers and sisters with whom she lived, as a Jew under Roman oppression, a poor and marginalized existence similar to the existence of Blacks in the Church for so long a time. They relate to her by sharing in her experiences as women who are also oppressed but who continue to bear the burden of faith and to pass on that faith to generations to come. At a time when women were supposed to be silent and invisible, when women were considered of little importance, Mary accepted a singular call from God to stand out as "blessed among all women" as a young, pregnant, unwed woman who would have many difficult questions to answer within her community but who had the courage to say a "yes" to God that shattered all of time. She is a role model, not for passivity, but for strong, righteous, "womanish" women who spend their lives giving birth to the future.

It is African American Catholic women who have been

the bearers and the preservers of their culture, of their heritage, of their faith, both Black and Catholic, and who have passed these treasures on to the next generations. It is they who have, through their abiding faith in a God who provides, a God who makes a way out of no way, provided Black Catholics, shunned by Black and white alike, with the courage and the strength to persevere.

Finally, Black Catholic womanists call upon the universal aspect of the Church and the holistic understanding of it which they share. As they look at the world today, they realize that as a people of color, they are not in the minority, nor are they a minority as a people of faith. Nor are they collectively, as women of all races, in the minority. That is the knowledge and the foundation upon which a womanist theology, inclusive of a Black Catholic womanist theology, must and can be built today.

In company with their Protestant sisters, they realize that all women must look at themselves, black, white, yellow, red and brown, and at each other, with new eyes reflective of the interconnectedness of our worlds today. Yet, they note that this must be done with eyes respective of the colorful diversity which makes of all humanity a "catholic" people.

Black Catholic womanist theology, like Black Catholic Theology, is still in the "birthing" process. It must be nurtured and sustained with the truths of our lives and the lives of those who have gone on before us as well as with the traditions of our faith heritage, as we have experienced and shared it, so that we can come to terms with the fullness of new life that will, in time, sustain and nurture us all.

Conclusion

At this time, Black Catholics are engaged in the development of a theology which will be Catholic in the deepest sense of that term. At the same time, as have all peoples before them, they seek to inculturate Catholic Christianity, imbuing it with the vitality and communitarianism which has enabled Black Catholics to remain faithful in a Church that has not always welcomed their presence. The Congress meetings have been a means of doing this, as they engage all Black Catholics at every level of the Church in a continuous and vibrant dialogue regarding what it means to be truly and authentically Black.[33]

The voices of those once invisible and unheard, Black Catholics, as well as Black women as seen in Chapter Seven, can and do provide a needed stimulus for rethinking the meaning and relevancy of Black Theology in the Christian Churches today. Their critique of Christianity, for its racism and sexism, and of Black culture, for its sexism, homophobia and growing classism, is of vital importance if we are to build a Christian Church of the future which lives up fully to the teachings of Jesus Christ.

Notes

1. For example, a recent major work on Black religion and the Black Churches, *The Black Church in the African American Experience* (Durham and London: Duke University Press, 1990), based on years of research and interviews of Black ministers, makes only brief reference to the Catholic Church and did not include Black priests (or Black women, Protestant or Catholic) as sources.

2. An excellent series of articles on those issues was presented in *The Tablet* (April 1994).

3. However, Black Catholics have engaged in the theological discussions since their beginning, as participants in the Civil Rights Movement and as members of the Black Theology Project of Theology in the Americas (see Cone, *Black Theology: A Documentary History, Volume 1:1966-1979* (Maryknoll, NY: Orbis, 1993), 2d ed. rev.). Tragically, two of the leading Black Catholic scholars died before they were able to present their theological perspectives in a systematic form. Fr. Bede Abrams, O.F.M.Conv., and Fr. Joseph Nearon, S.S.S., can be said to be among the founders of modern Black Catholic Theology. In 1978 the National Black Catholic Clergy Caucus sponsored a symposium proposed by Sr. Jamie Phelps, O.P., and Frs. Thaddeus Posey, Augustus Taylor, and David Benz, to bring together Black Catholic theologians, historians, clergy and religious. The proceedings were published as *Theology: A Portrait in Black* (Pittsburgh: NBCCC, 1980), edited by Fr. Posey. The symposium led to the founding of the Institute for Black Catholic Studies, now based at Xavier University (LA), the only Black Catholic university in the United States. In 1980 the first classes were held with Fr. Nearon, Sr. Thea Bowman, F.S.P.A., Sr. Toinette Eugene, Steve Wesley, Fr. Moses Anderson, S.S.E., and Fr. Cyprian Doris, O.S.B., as faculty. The Institute offers the Master of Theology in Pastoral Studies degree and certificate programs for Catechists, Youth Ministry, and Leadership. A second symposium was held in 1980 but the papers were not published. The symposium was reconstituted in 1991 and now meets annually. Its membership consists of Black theologians and scholars in related disciplines.

4. See Davis, *Black Catholics*, chapters 4, 6.

5. The first Black Catholic Congress was held in 1889, organized and led by lay Black leaders, such as Daniel Rudd, editor of the first national Black Catholic newspaper, and

others who raised their voices to protest the exclusion of Blacks in leadership roles in the Church and who proposed specific actions to be taken by the Catholic hierarchy to improve the situation of Black Catholics in the United States. See Cyprian Davis, *The History of Black Catholics in the United States* (N.Y.: Crossroad, 1990) for an in-depth presentation of the history of Black Catholics in this country, and also Shawn Copeland, O.P., "African American Catholics and Black Theology: An Interpretation," in James Cone and Gayraud Wilmore, eds., *Black Theology: A Documentary History*, Volume II (Maryknoll, NY: Orbis, 1993), pp. 99-115 for a discussion of the "pastoral and theological appropriation of Black Theology among African American Catholics."

6. Davis, *Black Catholics*, Chapter 1, pp. 1-27.

7. Raboteau, *Slave Religion*, Chapter 5, pp. 271-75, and Hayes, "Black Catholic Revivalism."

8. See Davis, *Black Catholics*, chapter 1.

9. "Black Spirituality: A Catholic Perspective," in *One Faith, One Lord, One Baptism: The Hopes and Experiences of the Black Community in the Archdiocese of New York*, Vol. 2 (N.Y.: Archdiocese of New York, 1988), p. 45.

10. John Paul II, "Address to Black Catholic Leadership in New Orleans," in *Unity in the Work of Service* (Washington, D.C.: U.S. Catholic Conference, 1987), p. 55.

11. See "What We Have Seen and Heard," especially pp. 4 and 15.

12. As noted in earlier chapters, Cone was critiqued for his apparent over-reliance on Karl Barth while other liberation theologians have revealed in their work the influence of their education in Eurocentric seminaries and institutions of learning both in the U.S. and overseas. This influence is

impossible to avoid but at the same time a critical awareness of it is necessary in order to do true contextual theology.

13. United States Catholic Conference, *Brothers and Sisters to Us: U.S. Bishops' Pastoral Letter on Racism in Our Day* (Washington, D.C.: USCC, 1979), p. 1.

14. Ibid.

15. Pope Paul VI, *The Pope Speaks* 14 (1969).

16. Rivers, *Spirit in Worship*, p. 8.

17. National Office for Black Catholics, *Black Perspectives on "Evangelization of the Modern World"* (Washington, D.C.: NOBC, 1974), p. 5.

18. Peter Schineller, *Handbook on Inculturation* (Mahwah, N.J.: Paulist Press, 1980).

19. See Anscar Chapungco, *Cultural Adaptation of the Liturgy* (Mahwah, N.J.: Paulist, 1982) and *Liturgies of the Future: The Process and Methods of Inculturation* (Mahwah, N.J.: Paulist, 1989).

20. Chapungco, *Cultural Adaptation*, p. 59.

21. Diana L. Hayes, "Lineamenta: Strangers and Sojourners No More," in *Origins* (1/3/1991, Vol. 20: No. 30), pp. 482-483.

22. See Hayes, "Black Catholic Revivalism," and Clarence Rivers, ed., *This Far by Faith: American Black Worship and Its African Roots* (Cincinnati: Stimuli, Inc., 1977), as well as Chapter Two of this work.

23. See Davis, *Black Catholics, Brothers and Sisters to Us*, and the Pontifical Commission on Peace and Justice, *The Church and Racism* (Washington, D.C.: United States Catholic Conference, 1990).

24. They are Fr. Edward Braxton, Diana L. Hayes, Jamie Phelps, O.P., M. Shawn Copeland, and Fr. Bryan Massengale.

25. Shawn Copeland, "African American Catholics and Black Theology: An Interpretation," in Cone/Wilmore, eds., *Black Theology: A Documentary History*, Volume II (Maryknoll, NY: Orbis, 1993), p. 110.

26. He is the author of *The Wisdom Community* (Mahwah, N.J.: Paulist, 1980), *The Faith Community: One, Holy, Catholic and Apostolic* (Notre Dame, Ind.: Ava Maria Press, 1990), and numerous articles.

27. The first such congress was held in Washington, D.C. in 1889. After five successful meetings it was suppressed, yet has re-emerged in this century as a vehicle for Black Catholics to engage in "God-talk." See the *U.S. Catholic Historian*, Vols. 5 (1986) and 7 (1988), as well as Davis, *Black Catholics*. The Congresses, which are now held every five years, are supplemented by regional and diocesan mini-congresses in the other years which have been instrumental in bringing about a greater level of self-consciousness and empowerment among Black Catholics regarding their history, roles and responsibilities in the Church. Other national gatherings, such as Rejoice! and Unity Explosion as well as the bi-annual Ministry in Black Communities and annual Pastoring in Black Communities weeklong conferences organized by the Black Catholic Congress Office, have also successfully enabled Black Catholics and others who minister in and with Black communities to expand their knowledge of Black history, culture and traditions.

28. A forthcoming work, edited by Diana L. Hayes and Cyprian Davis and including articles by Black Catholic theologians and their colleagues in related disciplines, will set forth in greater detail the evolution of a Black Catholic theology from a theological, ethical, anthropological, catechetical, and historical perspective.

29. See Hayes, "Black Catholic Revivalism."

30. See the Bishops' Committee on the Liturgy, National Conference of Catholic Bishops, *In Spirit and in Truth: Black Catholic Reflections on the Order of Mass* (Washington, D.C.: USCC Office for Publishing and Promotion Services, 1987), and the Secretariat for the Liturgy and Secretariat for Black Catholics, National Conference of Catholic Bishops, *Plenty Good Room: The Spirit and Truth of African American Catholic Worship* (Washington, D.C.: USCC Office for Publishing and Promotion Services, 1991).

31. Gay Wilentz, *Binding Cultures*.

32. See Hayes, "To Be Black, Catholic and Female," in *New Theology Review*, Volume 6, #2 (May 1993), pp. 55-62.

33. See Cyprian Davis, *Black Catholics*, and "Black Catholics in Nineteenth Century America" in *The U.S. Catholic Historian*, Volume 5/1, "The Black Catholic Experience" (1986), pp. 1-18 and also Volume 7/2, 3, "The Black Catholic Community, 1880-1987 (1988).

9

A Vision of the Future

This work has been an effort to show the development and progress of Black Liberation Theology in the United States. As such, it has presented the historical experience of African Americans and their will to survive. As with all theologies, Black Liberation Theology begins from within a context. It is from the particular context of a particular people that all theologies develop, whether that is recognized or not. We cannot be completely objective, yet we must be aware of and be able to articulate our subjectiveness. Today, we are witnesses to the myriad voices of African Americans, male and female, Protestant and Catholic, Christian and non-Christian,[1] ringing out in joyous celebration of their diversity and in the faith-filled hope of their coming together with Christians of every race and ethnicity in a universality which is truly reflective of who and whose they are.

The situation in the Christian Churches today is one fraught with problems which pose a challenge to those within its embrace. It is a challenge to be more than we are, for we are called to recognize our own vocation in Christ Jesus, the Liberator of all humanity. We can react to the oppression, whether of race, class or sex, simply by leaving the Church in frustrated anger and pain, as many have done, or we can remain and continue to serve as a "thorn" in its side, remembering that the institutional structure is, indeed, human, but that all of us, regardless of race, ethnicity or gender, as the People of God are the Church in its fullness.

The project is a multi-layered one and must, therefore, be approached on different levels. It calls for, on the one hand, individuals working in their communities for the betterment and empowerment of those communities, as is being done with Black and other liberation theologies but also, on the other hand, for these various communities to work together as Christians, recognizing and rejoicing in the challenges that difference brings while finding solidarity in the mutual struggle and shared faith. The task, in other words, is holistic rather than dualistic. The development of Black Theology does not and should not take place at the expense of other equally liberating and liberated theologies for we must, in all reality, learn to survive and work together for the betterment of all. Thus, the call is also for further ecumenical dialogue with the many African Americans who have chosen other religious paths to follow but who are still very much a vital part of the Black community.

Black Theology challenges all of us "to [not] ignore our differences, or to view them as causes for separation and suspicion" but to see them "as forces for change."[2] It is the challenge that lies before all people of good will, regardless of race, class, gender or religion, to see with newly opened eyes the reality of the lives of Black women and men and to accept those differences which do and must exist as cause for celebration, not fear which leads only to prejudice and discrimination. We must constantly call to mind that it is by the one and same God that we were created in our diversity, thereby affirming the goodness of that creation.

The theology of the Black experience which has been set forth in the above pages is, in many ways, a call to metanoia for all Christians, not just a change of heart and mind but a complete revision of one's life in response to God. In its delineation of and meshing of the historical experience of Black America, Black Theology truly serves as a "classic" theological undertaking, one which serves as a paradigm for all future theologizing, for it has withstood the tests of time and the doubts of those who saw it merely as a "passing fad." Black Theology has survived and continues to develop because it is a living theology which has emerged from a vital and vibrant community committed to more than mere survival alone.

Black Theology has become a viable vehicle for presenting the true story of the survival and progress of a people who have been historically dismissed from public and historical view in the United States.

The second generation of Black theologians, a larger and more diverse group than the pioneering one, continues to struggle with the questions, needs, and concerns raised within the growing Black community in the United States and their efforts to continue the centuries-long dialogue with a God "who saves," while also addressing the challenges which continue to confront it, especially the continuing denial or distortion of the Black experience.

In reference to the events of 1992 in Los Angeles, Cornell West has noted:

> What happened in Los Angeles was neither a race riot nor a class rebellion. Rather this monumental upheaval was a multi-racial, trans-class, and largely male display of justified social rage. For all its ugly, xenophobic resentment, its air of adolescent carnival, and its downright barbaric behavior, it signified the sense of powerlessness in American society.... What we witnessed in Los Angeles

was the consequence of a lethal linkage of economic decline, cultural decay, and political lethargy in American life. Race was the visible catalyst, not the underlying cause.[3]

The result of falling into the trap of seeing race as the only issue affecting Black Americans today, which too many Americans regardless of race or ethnicity have done, is that Blacks become the "problem" people who are seen as never being satisfied regardless of what is *done for* them. Little attention is given to the humanity behind this "problem," even less to innovative ways of seeking to resolve the "problem" by going beyond it to see the harsh reality of a people still trapped by stereotype and false consciousness.

The Black community, and therefore Black Theology for which that community is both foundation and ever-renewing source, is facing an uncertain future, assaulted as it is on every side, disintegrating from a variety of forces, both internal and external, losing its self-understanding as a place of growth, vitality and renewal for Black peoples who, instead, are losing faith in each other, in their institutions, and in themselves.

The fault for this, obviously, cannot all be laid at the feet of Black Theology but, as the articulated voice of the people, it is in danger of falling captive to academia, a captivity which if it continues will not only reduce its ability to learn from and be enriched by the theologizing of the people at the lowest levels of Black society in the United States but will also nullify its efforts to reach out to and communicate with Black Americans in a manner and form which is intelligible to them.

As has been shown throughout this work, Black Theology is a grassroots theology, one which has challenged the status quo, especially that of academic theology with its Eurocentric mindset. Increasingly today, Black Theology has become an accepted part of the curriculum of institutions of higher learning while workshops and seminars at theological conferences have proliferated. The question that must be raised is whether, in so doing, the revolutionary stance and historical challenge of Black Theology will be nullified and co-opted by an academic agenda as more Black theologians attempt to do what is required to acquire tenure and promotion. Hopefully this will not be the case, but to ensure that it is not, Black theologians must consciously and continually make the effort to straddle, as in actuality African Americans have always been required to do, the worlds of academia and the Black community. If those ties are lost, Black Theology will simply become another "top-down" ideology doomed to eventual obsolescence. There is a need therefore for constant re-evaluation and constructive self-critique of Black Theology by Black theologians on all levels, whether based in the academy or nurtured in the black community.

Continuing efforts to dialogue with ordinary Black Christians from every walk of life, Protestant, Catholic and Orthodox, must be made, not in lecture halls alone but in their churches, their neighborhoods and their homes as well.

One of the most striking paradoxes, for many, that took place after the Rodney King beating and the subsequent urban uprising in Los Angeles was the seeming silence on the part of the Christian Churches as a whole, including the Black Church. This is not to say that individual churches, ministers, congregations, and even theologians were not involved in efforts to deal with the myriad issues arising from those events, but, to date, seemingly few concerted efforts on national or regional levels, to my knowledge, other than conferences and dialogues, have taken place which would bring the concerted force of the Church into play. The historical role of the Black Church as source of revolutionary renewal and challenge is being lost along with the futures of our children, few of whom have any regular contact with the institutional Church anymore.

Black Americans have, like their fellow Americans, become increasingly seduced by the trappings of secular society to the extent that they are losing contact with the holistic sense of themselves as a community bound together by ties that go beyond simple blood lines to encompass a shared struggle to survive and get ahead. They see the role of Black faith as an increasingly passive one rather than the historically assertive voice for change that it has been as channeled through the Black Churches. As Stephen Carter noted, speaking with regard to the entire country:

> In our sensible zeal to keep religion from dominating our politics, we have created a political and legal culture that presses the religiously faithful to be other than themselves, to act publicly, and sometimes privately as well, as though their faith does not matter to them.[4]

While the numbers of illegitimate births, divorces and impoverished female-headed households continue to escalate in the Black community, so does the number of Blacks who acknowledge no affiliation with any type or form of organized religion, especially those between the ages of fifteen and thirty-five. An entire generation is being lost to the Church and to the Black community as a whole, their lives cut short by inferior education, incarceration, poverty, and death, either self-inflicted or inflicted by someone from their own neighborhood. We, those privileged because of education and good jobs, seem unable and too often unwilling to stop the hemorrhaging of our life's blood. The Church and religion, in any form, has become irrelevant, replaced by a seemingly willful desire toward self-destruction, witnessed in the rising death toll on our inner-city streets. Getting ahead is no longer seen in terms of obtaining a good education and a good job which enables you to return something to the community from which you were sent. Rather, it is buying a fancy car and a big house, and having a high-paying job, either in the legitimate or illegitimate world. Our youth have become co-opted by American cultural values which place more of an emphasis on competition and the profit motive rather than on solidarity, compromise and sacrifice and whose icons are money, profit and greed rather than the family, the community and God.

The Black Church is all too often out of touch with Black theologians, and both have seemingly lost contact with the grassroots people who are necessarily the source of our theologizing and the Black Church's very existence. The Church has become isolated within the Black community, concerned too often with building bigger edifices or moving to the suburbs to join their upwardly mobile parishioners; they work only with those already within their walls, fearful of reaching out to those outside, the increasingly desperate and hopeless Black poor. Black theologians find themselves, willingly or unwillingly, caught up in the hectic pace of academic life or Church pastoring, presentation of scholarly papers or books, committee and board meetings, with little time to talk with or, more importantly, listen to the cries of the people trapped within a seemingly endless round of desperation and despair.

The question James Cone asked in the late 1960s must be rephrased and raised once again: Has Christianity and the Christian God, especially its Black expression, become irrelevant and superfluous to the needs of an increasingly irreligious Black community, if we can even talk in terms of one Black community any longer?[5] Is it in danger of or has it already become simply another bourgeois ideology which pacifies its members but does not challenge them to concerted action on behalf of their own?

The answer must be no, but a "no" hedged with conditions. For Black Christianity to remain viable, it must reimmerse itself in the ebb and flow of the life of the Black community as a whole, with all of the problems that immersion will bring. The Black Church, as the institution reflective of that faith, and Black theologians, as articulators of its vision, must be about the business of rebuilding the lives and spirits of Black Americans, churched and unchurched, and, equally important, must reaffirm its catalytic role in American society as a sign of contradiction to the complacent and sterile lives so many live today. Despite the many negative signs, hope still exists, and where there is hope, there is faith.

A common path must be forged across lines of conservative and liberal, progressive and moderate, middle and lower as well as upper class, male or female, and even Christian, Muslim or other faiths. We must return to that age-old understanding of Blacks as a people who may and can disagree internally but who stand united as a people against a common foe: racism which takes on so many forms in this country.

At the same time, we must reach across barriers, falsely erected, to those others who have been historically oppressed in the United States because of their race, ethnicity, native tongue, gender or class. In order to profitably survive and thrive, African Americans must work in solidarity with Hispanic, Native, Asian and other Americans, both male and female. Only in this way will we be able to take advantage of the changing demographics of this nation which reveal that the so called "minorities" are in actuality rapidly becoming the majority if they will only unite. In the Roman Catholic Church, this is especially critical as the face of the Church changes to that of a person of color who is predominantly Spanish-speaking. This shift provides a "kairotic" moment, a window of opportunity opened in God's time rather than that of humanity, to begin to forge new ties with others whose cultures and traditions may differ but whose experiences of oppression have much in common, leading to the emergence of their own liberating theologies.

The dialogues which Black theologians are and have been engaged in with proponents of these liberating theologies throughout the United States and the world are critical and must continue, enabling the dialogue to expand and reach out to more and more of those affected by the trend toward "blaming the victim" which is once again rearing its ugly head. These dialogues have mutually raised consciousness of the multiplicative impact of race, class and gender oppression throughout the world, revealing, thereby, the necessity of dealing with these "isms" as a whole rather than one by one. Ties with other peoples and nations must be encouraged as we seek to strengthen the bonds that bring us together while honoring the differences that make us uniquely who we are.

Black liberation theology is continuing to develop in new and different ways. New works which address more critically the issues of the Black community, this nation and global society as a whole are appearing regularly, as seen in this text. These works run the gamut from issues of family wholeness to ethics to Black Theology's role in the public arena while also addressing the historical questions of theology concerning God, Jesus Christ and the Church.[6]

As we move forward into the twenty-first century, new issues and concerns arise, such as the resurgence of racism in American society, the growth of a Black conservatism and the forces of the religious right, the continuing sexism and homophobia of the Black Church and community and the renewed assault on "gains" fought for and thought won during and after the Civil Rights Movement such as Affirmative Action, Voting Rights, Welfare Rights, etc.

Black theologians must be involved in these issues; they must continue to serve as the "mediators" of the Black community, listening to the issues and concerns raised from within its midst and articulating them in ways that cannot be ignored by those on any level in society today. People once thought incapable of profound speech, or coherent speech at all, are speaking out in diverse ways on issues which challenge their continued existence in this land. Black theologians, by their ties with the people, with academia, with both federal and local government, and other venues, can and must serve to ensure that these voices will never more be silenced or ignored.

The new generations of Black theologians, male and female, as well as those who laid the groundwork for what has become a truly liberating and liberated theology, are certainly up to the task that is set before them. In their new works, they continue to learn from the past while looking ahead to the future, preaching and prophesying for all. More laborers are needed in the Lord's vineyard to take up the task, for the more we explore, the more we uncover that needs to be done. As we enter into the third millennium of the Christian faith, Black Theology looks ahead to a future that is full of challenges but also bright with hope-filled possibilities. African Americans have been a people whose minds were "set on freedom" but whose spirit encompassed all who came within their community and provided, with the help of God, sustenance for the journey. That journey is not yet over, but our eyes are still "watching God" and our minds are still set on freedom. It will come.

Notes

1. An area for fruitful further exploration must be the theologies emerging from the Islamic movement and Buddhists in the Black community, the challenges they present to the historical understanding of African Americans as a Christian people and the avenues for ecumenical dialogue and shared development within the Black community.

2. "The Master's Tools Will Never Dismantle the Master's House," in *Sister, Outsider: Essays and Speeches* (Freedom, Ca.: The Crossing Press, 1984), p. 112.

3. "Race Matters" in Gooding-Williams, *Reading Rodney King / Reading Urban Uprising*, p. 255.

4. *The Culture of Disbelief: How American Law and Politics Trivialize Religious Devotion* (New York: Basic Books, 1993), p. 3.

5. See Henry Louis Gates, "Two Nations...Both Black," in Gooding-Williams, ed., *Reading Rodney King, Reading Urban Uprising*, pp. 249-254.

6. Other works not already mentioned which have recently been published include Marcia Y. Riggs, *Awake, Arise and Act:*

A Womanist Call for Black Liberation (Cleveland: The Pilgrim Press, 1995); J. Deotis Roberts, *The Prophethood of Black Believers: An African American Political Theology for Ministry* (1995); Robert Hood, *Black and Begrimed* (Minneapolis: Fortress Press, 1995); Karen Baker-Fletcher, *A Singing Something: Anna J. Cooper and the Foundations of Womanist Theology* (New York: Crossroad, 1994); Mary Sawyer, *Black Ecumenism: Implementing the Demands of Justice* (Valley Forge, Pa.: Trinity Press International, 1994), and many others yet in progress. Many of the above and those forthcoming address some of the issues raised in this final chapter regarding the continuing role of Black Theology and the Black Church in the Black community.

Select Bibliography

Abrahams, Roger D., ed. *Afro-American Folk Tales: Stories from Black Traditions in the New World.* New York: Pantheon Books, 1985.

Ashe, Arthur, assisted by Kip Branch et al. *A Hard Road to Glory—Track and Field: The African American Athlete in Track and Field.* New York: Amistad Press, 1988, reprinted 1993.

Bailey, Randall, and Jacqueline Grant, eds. *The Recovery of Black Presence: An Interdisciplinary Exploration.* Nashville: Abingdon Press, 1995.

Baker-Fletcher, Garth Kasimu. *Somebodyness: Martin Luther King, Jr. and the Theory of Dignity.* Minneapolis: Fortress Press, 1993.

_____. *Xodus: An African-American Male Journey.* Minneapolis: Fortress Press, 1995.

Baker-Fletcher, Karen. *A Singing Something: Anna J. Cooper and the Foundations of Womanist Theology.* New York: Crossroad, 1994.

Baldwin, Lewis. *There Is a Balm in Gilead: The Cultural Roots of Martin Luther King, Jr.* Minneapolis: Fortress Press, 1991.

_____. *To Make the Wounded Whole: The Cultural Legacy of Martin Luther King, Jr.* Minneapolis: Fortress Press, 1992.

Barbour, Floyd B., ed. *The Black Power Revolt.* Boston: Beacon, 1968.

Bennett, Lerone. *Before the Mayflower: A History of Black America.* New York: Penguin Books, 1993, 6th ed. rev.

Bernal, Martin. *Black Athena: The Afroasiatic Roots of Classical Civilization*, 2 vols. New Brunswick: Rutgers University Press, v. 1, 1987; v. 2, 1991.

Berry, Mary, and John W. Blassingame. *Long Memory: The Black Experience in America*. New York and Oxford: Oxford University Press, 1982.

Bevans, Stephen. *Models of a Contextual Theology*. Maryknoll: Orbis, 1992.

Bishops' Committee on the Liturgy, National Conference of Catholic Bishops. *In Spirit and in Truth: Black Catholic Reflections on the Order of Mass*. Washington, D.C.: USCC Office for Publishing and Promotion Services, 1987.

Black Bishops of the United States, *What We Have Seen and Heard: A Pastoral Letter on Evangelization*. Cincinnati: St. Anthony Messenger Press, 1984

Branch, Taylor. *Parting the Waters: America in the King Years, 1954–1963*. New York: Simon and Schuster, 1988.

Braxton, Edward. *The Wisdom Community*. Mahwah: Paulist, 1980.

_____. *The Faith Community: One, Holy, Catholic and Apostolic*. Notre Dame: Ave Maria Press, 1990.

Breitman, George, ed. *By Any Means Necessary*. New York: Pathfinder Press, 1970.

_____, ed. *Malcolm X Speaks*. New York: Grove Press, 1965.

Brooks, Walter. "The Priority of the Silver Bluff Church and Its Promoters" in *The Journal of Negro History* 7/1922.

Cannon, Katie. *Black Womanist Ethics*. Atlanta: Scholars Press, 1988.

_____. *Katie's Canon: Womanism and the Soul of the Black Community*. New York: Continuum, 1995.

Carson, Clayborne, et al., eds. *The Papers of Martin Luther King, Jr.* vol. 1. *Called To Serve*. Berkeley: University of California Press, 1992.

_____. *In Struggle: SNCC and the Black Awakening of the 1960's*. Cambridge: Harvard University Press, 1981.

Carter, Harold. *The Prayer Tradition of Black People*. Baltimore: Gateway Press, 1982.

Carter, Stephen. *The Culture of Disbelief: How American Law and Politics Trivialize Religious Devotion*. New York: Basic Books, 1993.

Chapungco, Anscar. *Cultural Adaptation of the Liturgy*. Mahwah: Paulist, 1982.

_____. *Liturgies of the Future: The Process and Methods of Inculturation*. Mahwah: Paulist, 1989.

Clark, Erskine. *Wrestlin' Jacob: A Portrait of Religion in the Old South*. Atlanta: John Knox Press, 1979.

Cleage, Albert. *The Black Messiah*. New York: Sheed and Ward, 1968.

_____. *Black Christian Nationalism: New Directions for the Black Church*. New York: Morrow, 1972.

Collins, Patricia Hill. *Black Feminist Thought: Knowledge, Consciousness, and the Politics of Empowerment*. New York: Routledge, 1991, vol. 2, *Perspectives on Gender*.

Conde, Maryse. *Sequ*. New York: Ballantine Books, 1988.

_____. *The Children of Sequ*. New York: Ballantine Books, 1990.

Cone, Cecil. *The Identity Crisis in Black Theology*. Nashville: The African Methodist Episcopal Church, 1975.

Cone, James. *A Black Theology of Liberation*. Philadelphia: Lippincott, 1970; reprint 1986; 20th anniversary ed., Maryknoll: Orbis, 1990.

_____. *Black Theology and Black Power*. New York: Seabury Press, 1969; reprint 1986; 20th anniversary ed., New York: Harper & Row, 1989.

_____ and Gayraud Wilmore, eds. *Black Theology: A Documentary History*, vol. 1, 1966-1979, 2d ed. rev., 1993; vol. 2, 1980-1992. Maryknoll: Orbis Books, 1993.

_____. *For My People: Black Theology and the Black Church*. Maryknoll: Orbis Books, 1984.

_____. *God of the Oppressed*. New York: Seabury Press, 1975.

_____. *Martin, Malcolm and America: A Dream or a Nightmare?* Maryknoll: Orbis, 1992.

_____. *My Soul Looks Back*. Nashville: Abingdon Press, 1982, Journeys of Faith series, Robert A. Raines, ed.; republished Maryknoll: Orbis Books, 1986.

_____. *Speaking the Truth: Ecumenism, Liberation and Black Theology*. Grand Rapids: Eerdmans, 1986.

_____. *The Spirituals and the Blues*. New York: Seabury Press, 1972; reprint 1991, Maryknoll: Orbis Books.

Copher, Charles B. *Black Biblical Studies: An Anthology of Charles B. Copher: Biblical and Theological Issues on the Black Presence in the Bible*. Chicago: Black Light Fellowship, 1993.

Davidson, Basil. *Modern Africa: A Social and Political History*, 2nd ed. White Plains: Longman, 1993.

_____. *Black Man's Burden: Africa and the Curse of the Nation State*. New York: Times Books, 1992.

_____. *African Civilization Revisited: From Antiquity to Modern Times*, 2nd rev. ed. Trenton: African World Press, 1990.

_____. *Africa in History*, rev. ed. New York: Macmillan, 1990.

_____. *The African Genius: An Introduction to Social and Cultural History*. New York: Little Brown, 1989.

_____. *The Lost Cities of Africa*, rev. ed. New York: Little Brown, 1988.

_____. *The African Slave Trade*, rev. ed. New York: Little Brown, 1988.

_____. *The Lost Cities of Africa*. Boston: Little, Brown and Co., 1987, rev. ed..

_____. *Let Freedom Come: Africa in Modern History*. New York: Little Brown, 1979.

Davis, Cyprian. "Black Catholics in Nineteenth Century America" in *The U.S. Catholic Historian*, Volume 5/1, "The Black Catholic Experience," 1986, pp. 1-18.

_____. "Black Spirituality: A Catholic Perspective" in *One Faith, One Lord, One Baptism: The Hopes and Experiences of the Black Community in the Archdiocese of New York*, vol. 2. New York: Archdiocese of New York, 1988, p. 45.

_____ "The Black Catholic Community" in *The U.S. Catholic Historian*, vol. 7/2, 3, 1880-1987, 1988.

_____. *The History of Black Catholics in the United States*. New York: Crossroad, 1990.

Delany, Martin R. *The Condition, Elevation, and Destiny of the Colored People of the United States, Politically Considered.* Salem: Ayer Press, rep. of 1852 ed.

Diop, Cheikh Ante. *Civilization or Barbarism: An Authentic Anthropology*, Harold J. Salemson, and Marjolin Dejager, eds. Chicago: Lawrence Hill Books, 1991.

_____. *The Cultural Unity of Black Africa*, 2nd ed. Chicago: Third World Press, 1987.

_____. *Precolonial Black Africa*. Chicago: Lawrence Hill Books, 1987.

_____. *The African Origins of Civilization: Myth or Reality.* Chicago: Lawrence Hill Books, 1974; originally published, Paris: Presence Africaine, 1967.

Dolan, Jay P. *Catholic Revivalism: The American Experience, 1830-1900*. Notre Dame: Notre Dame Press, 1978.

_____. *The American Catholic Experience*. Garden City: Doubleday and Co., 1985.

_____. "American Catholics and Revival Religion, 1850-1900" in *Horizons* 3, Spring 1976.

Dornisch, Loretta. "Symbolic Systems and the Interpretation of Scripture" in *Semeia* 4, 1975.

Douglas, Kelly Brown. *The Black Christ*. Maryknoll: Orbis, 1994.

DuBois, W.E.B. "The Talented Tenth" in Deirdre Mullane, ed., *Crossing the Danger Water*. New York: Anchor Doubleday, 1993.

_____. "Of Mr. Booker T. Washington and Others" in *The Souls of Black Folk*. New York: Literary Classics of the United States, 1986.

Dulles, Avery. *Models of Revelation*. Garden City: Doubleday, 1983; first published by Harper and Row, 1957.

Early, Gerald, ed. *Lure and Loathing: Essays on Race, Identity, and the Ambivalence of Assimilation*. New York: Penguin Books, 1993.

Egbulem, Chris Nwaka. *The Power of Africentric Celebrations*: *Inspirations from the Zairean Liturgy*. New York: Crossroad, 1995.

Epps, Archie, ed. *The Speeches of Malcolm X at Harvard*. New York: William Morrow, 1968.

_____. *Malcolm X on Afro-American History*. New York: Pathfinder Press, 1970.

Eugene, Toinette with James Newton Poling, *Balm for Gilead: Pastoral Advocacy for African American Families Experiencing Abuse*. Nashville: Abingdon Press, 1995.

_____. *Lifting As We Climb: A Womanist Ethic of Care*. Nashville: Abingdon Press, forthcoming.

Evans, James. *We Have Been Believers: An African American Systematic Theology*. Minneapolis: Fortress Press, 1993.

Felder, Cain. *Troubling Biblical Waters: Race, Class and Family*. Maryknoll: Orbis, 1989.

_____, ed. *Stony the Road We Trod: African American Biblical Interpretation*. Minneapolis: Fortress Press, 1991.

Finney, Charles G. "What a Revival of Religion Is" in *Lecture on Revivals of Religion*. Cambridge: Belknap Press of Harvard University Press, 1960.

Franklin, John Hope. *Racial Equality in America*. Columbia: University of Missouri Press, 1993.

_____. *The Color Line: Legacy for the 21st Century*. Columbia: University of Missouri Press, 1993.

_____ and Alfred Moss, Jr. *From Slavery To Freedom: A History of Negro Americans*. New York: Alfred J. Knopf, 1987, 6th ed.

Frazier, E. Franklin and C. Eric Lincoln. *The Negro Church in America and The Black Church in America Since Frazier*. New York: Schocken Books, 1974.

Gallen, David, ed. *A Malcolm X Reader: Perspectives on the Man and the Myths*. New York: Carroll and Graf, 1994.

Garnet, Henry Highland. "An Address to the Slaves of the United States of America," 1843 in Mullane, op. cit.

Gates, Henry Louis. *Colored People*. New York: Oxford University Press, 1994.

_____. *Loose Canons: Notes on the Culture Wars*. New York: Oxford University Press, 1992.

_____. *Bearing Witness: Selections from African American*

Autobiography in the Twentieth Century. New York: Pantheon Press, 1991.

_____. *Reading Black, Reading Feminist: A Critical Anthology*. New York: Dutton, 1990.

_____. *Figures in Black: Words, Signs and the "Racial" Self*. New York: Oxford University Press, 1989.

_____, ed. *Spiritual Narratives: M.W. Stewart, J. Lee, J.A.J. Foote, V.W. Broughton* and *Amanda Smith, An Autobiography: The Story of the Lord's Dealings with Mrs A. Smith, the Colored Evangelist*. New York: Oxford University Press, 1988.

_____. *The Signifying Monkey: A Theory of African American Literary Criticism*. New York: Oxford University Press, 1988.

Genovese, Eugene D. *From Rebellion to Revolution: Afro-American Slave Revolts in the Making of the Modern World*. Baton Rouge: Louisiana State University Press, 1979.

Giddings, Paula. *When and Where I Enter: The Impact of Black Women on Race and Sex in America*. New York: William Morrow, 1984.

Gooding-Williams, Robert, ed. *Reading Rodney King, Reading Urban Uprising*. New York: Routledge, 1993.

Grant, Jacquelyn. *White Woman's Christ, Black Woman's Jesus*. Atlanta: Scholars Press, 1989.

Hacker, Andrew. *Two Nations: Black and White, Separate, Hostile, Unequal*. New York: Charles Scribner's Sons, 1992.

Hamilton, Virginia. *The People Could Fly: American Black Folktales*. New York: Alfred P. Knopf, 1985.

Harding, Vincent. *There Is a River: The Black Struggle for Freedom in America*. New York and London: Harcourt Brace Jovanovich, 1981.

_____ *Hope and History: Why We Must Share the Story of the Movement*. Maryknoll: Orbis, 1990.

Hayes, Diana L. "Slain in the Spirit: Black Americans and the Holy Spirit" in *The Journal of the Interdenominational Theological Center*, vol. XX, #1/2, Fall 1992/Spring 1993.

_____. "To Be Black, Catholic and Female" in *New Theology Review*, vol. 6, #2, May 1993, pp. 55-62.

_____. "Tracings of an American Theology" in *Louvain Studies* 14/4, Winter 1989.

_____. *"Lineamenta: Strangers and Sojourners No More"* in *Origins* 1/3/1991, vol. 20: no. 30, pp. 482-483.

_____. *Trouble Don't Last Always: Soul Prayers*. Collegeville: The Liturgical Press, 1995..

_____. *Hagar's Daughters: Womanist Ways of Being in the World*. Mahwah: Paulist Press, 1995.

_____. *And Still We Rise: An Introduction to Black Liberation Theology*. Mahwah: Paulist Press, 1996.

_____. "Black Catholic Revivalism: The Emergence of a New Form of Worship" in *The Journal of the Interdenominational Theological Center*, Vol. 14, Fall 1986/Spring 1987.

Herskovits, Melville J. *The Myth of the Negro Past*. Boston: Beacon Press, 1958.

Higginbotham, Evelyn Brooks. *Righteous Discontent: The Women's Movement in the Black Baptist Church, 1880-1920*. Cambridge: Harvard University Press, 1993.

Hine, Darlene Clark, ed. *Black Women in America: An Historical Encyclopedia*. Brooklyn: Carlson Publishing, 1993.

Hood, Robert. *Begrimed and Black*. Minneapolis: Fortress Press, 1995.

_____. *Must God Remain Greek? Afro Cultures and God Talk*. Minneapolis: Fortress Press, 1990.

Hooks, Bell. *Killing Rage*. New York: Henry Holt, 1995.

_____. *Outlaw Culture: Resisting Representations*. New York: Routledge, 1994.

_____. *Teaching to Transgress: Education and the Practice of Freedom*. New York: Routledge, 1994.

_____. *Black Looks: Race and Representation*. Boston: South End Press, 1992.

_____ and Cornel West. *Breaking Bread: Insurgent Black Intellectual Life*. Boston: South End Press, 1991.

_____. *Yearning: Race, Gender and Cultural Politics*. Boston: South End Press, 1990.

_____. *Talking Back: Thinking Feminist, Thinking Black*. Boston: South End Press, 1989.

_____. *Feminist Theory: From Margin to Center*. Boston: South End Press, 1984.

_____. *Ain't I a Woman? Black Women and Feminism*. Boston: South End Press, 1981.

Hopkins, Dwight and George Cummings, eds. *Cut Loose Your Stammering Tongues: Black Theology and the Slave Narratives*. Maryknoll: Orbis, 1992.

_____. *Black Theology: United States and South Africa*. Maryknoll: Orbis, 1989.

_____ *Shoes That Fit Our Feet: Sources for a Constructive Black Theology*. Maryknoll: Orbis, 1993.

Hurston, Zora Neale. *Mules and Men*. Philadelphia: J.B. Lippincott, 1935; republished 1990, New York: Harper and Row.

_____. *The Sanctified Church*, ed. by Toni Cade Bambara. Berkeley: Turtle Island Foundation, 1981.

_____. *Tell My Horse*. Philadelphia: J.B. Lippincott, 1938; republished 1990, New York: Harper and Row.

_____. *Their Eyes Were Watching God*. New York: Harper and Row, 1990, originally published, 1937.

Jackson, Luther P. "Religious Instruction of Negroes, 1830 to 1860, with Special Reference to South Carolina" in *Journal of Negro History* 15, January 1930.

Jackson, Rebecca. *Gifts of Power: The Writings of Rebecca Jackson, Black Visionary, Shaker Eldress*. Amherst: University of Massachusetts Press, 1981.

John Paul II, "Address to Black Catholic Leadership in New Orleans" in *Unity in the Work of Service*. Washington, D.C.: U.S. Catholic Conference, 1987.

Johnson, Clifton, ed. *God Struck Me Dead: Voices of the Ex-Slaves*. Cleveland: Pilgrim Press, 1993; originally published, 1969.

Johnson, Elizabeth. *She Who Is: The Mystery of God in Feminist Theological Discourse*. New York: The Crossroad Publishing Company, 1992.

Jones, Arthur. *Wade in the Water: The Wisdom of the Spirituals*. Maryknoll: Orbis, 1993.

Jones, Major. *Black Awareness: A Theology of Hope*. Nashville: Abingdon Press, 1971.

_____. *Black Christian Ethics*. Nashville: Abingdon Press, 1974.

_____. *The Color of God: The Concept of God in Afro-American Thought*. Macon: Mercer University Press, 1987.

Jones, William. *Is God a White Racist? A Preamble to Black Theology*. Garden City: Anchor Press/Doubleday, 1973.

Jordan, Winthrop D. *White Over Black: American Attitudes Toward the Negro, 1550-1812*. Baltimore: Penguin Press, 1968.

Joseph, Gloria I., and Jill Lewis. *Common Differences: Conflicts in Black and White Feminist Perspectives*. Boston: South End Press, 1981.

King, Martin Luther, Jr. *Testament of Hope: The Essential Writings of Martin Luther King, Jr.*, Jas. M. Washington, ed. New York: Harper and Row, 1986.

_____. *Stride Toward Freedom: The Montgomery Story*, 1958, republished San Francisco: Harper San Francisco, 1987.

_____. *The Strength To Love*, 1963; republished Minneapolis: Augsburg Fortress, 1981.

_____. *The Trumpet of Conscience*, 1967, republished San Francisco: Harper San Francisco, 1989.

_____. *Where Do We Go From Here: Chaos or Community?* Boston: Beacon Press, 1967.

_____. *Why We Can't Wait*, 1964; republished New York: Dutton, 1993.

Kunnie, Julian. *Models of Black Theology: Issues in Class, Culture, and Gender*. Valley Forge: Trinity Press International, 1994.

Lawrence, Charles R. "The Separated Darker Brethren" in *Christianity and Crisis* 25, February 22, 1965.

Lerner, Gerda, ed. *Black Women in White America: A Documentary History*. New York: Vintage, 1973.

Levine, Lawrence. *Black Culture and Black Consciousness*. New York: Oxford University Press, 1977.

Lincoln, C. Eric and Lawrence Mamiya. *The Black Church in*

the *African American Experience*. Durham and London: Duke University Press, 1990.

_____. *Race, Religion and the Continuing American Dilemma*. New York: Hill and Wang, 1986.

Long, Jerome H. "Review of *Black Religion* by Joseph R. Washington," *Foundations* 7, October 1964.

Lorde, Audre. "The Master's Tools Will Never Dismantle the Master's House" in *Sister, Outsider: Essays and Speeches*. Freedom: The Crossing Press, 1984.

Lowell, John. *Black Song: The Forge and the Flame*. New York: Paragon House, 1986.

Maas, Robin, and Gabriel O'Donnell, O.P. *Spiritual Traditions for the Contemporary Church*. Nashville: Abingdon Press, 1990.

Malcom X. *February 1965: The Final Speeches*, Steve Clark, ed. New York: Pathfinder Press, 1992.

_____. *By Any Means Necessary*, rev. ed. New York: Pathfinder Press, 1992.

_____. *Malcolm X Speaks*, 2nd ed. New York: Pathfinder Press, 1989.

_____. *Malcolm X on Afro-American History*, 3rd ed. New York: Pathfinder Press, 1967.

_____. *The Autobiography of Malcolm X*, Alex Haley, ed. New York: Grove Press, 1965.

Marable, Manning. *The Crisis of Color and Democracy: Essays on Race, Class and Power*. Monroe: Common Courage, 1992.

_____. *Race, Reform and Rebellion: The Second Reconstruction in Black America, 1945-1990*, 2nd rev. ed. Jackson: University Press of Mississippi, 1991.

_____. *How Capitalism Underdeveloped Black America*. Boston: South End Press, 1983.

_____. *Blackwater: Historical Studies in Race, Class Consciousness, and Revolution*. Dayton: Black Praxis Press, 1981.

Martey, Emmanuel. *African Theology: Inculturation and Liberation*. Maryknoll: Orbis, 1993.

Mays, Benjamin. *The Negro's God as Reflected in His Literature*. Greenwood Pr., 1970, originally published, 1938.

Mbiti, John S. *African Religions and Philosophy*. Garden City: Doubleday Anchor Books, 1970.

McLoughlin, William G. *Revivals, Awakenings and Reform: An Essay on Religion and Social Change in America, 1607-1977*. Chicago: University of Chicago Press, 1978.

Metz, Johann Baptist. *Faith in History and Society: Toward a Practical Fundamental Theology*. New York: Crossroad, 1980.

Mills, Kay. *This Little Light of Mine: The Life of Fannie Lou Hamer*. New York: Dutton, 1993.

Mitchell, Henry, and Nicholas Lewter. *Black Belief*. New York: Harper and Row, 1975.

_____. *Black Preaching*. New York: Harper and Row, 1970.

_____. *Soul Theology: The Heart of American Black Culture*. Nashville: Abingdon, 1991.

_____. *Black Preaching*. Philadelphia: Lippincott, 1970.

Mosala, Itumeleng. *The Unquestionable Right To Be Free: Black Theology from South Africa*. Maryknoll: Orbis, 1986.

Moyd, Olin P. "The Old-Time Revival" in *Freeing the Spirit* II, Summer 1973.

Mudge, Lewis S., ed. *Essays on Biblical Interpretation*. Philadelphia: Fortress Press, 1980.

Mullane, Deirdre, ed. *Crossing the Danger Water: Three Hundred Years of African American Writing*. New York: Anchor Doubleday, 1993.

National Conference of Catholic Bishops, *Brothers and Sisters to Us: A Pastoral Letter on Racism*. Washington, D.C.: United States Catholic Conference, 1974.

National Office for Black Catholics, *Black Perspectives on "Evangelization of the Modern World."* Washington, D.C.: NOBC, 1974.

Ochs, Stephen. *Desegregating the Altar: The Josephites and the Struggle for Black Priests, 1871-1960*. Baton Rouge: Louisiana State University Press, 1990.

Paris, Peter J. *The Spirituality of African Peoples: The Search for a Common Moral Discourse*. Minneapolis: Augsburg Fortress, 1995.

Payne, Wardell J., ed. *Directory of African American Religious*

Bodies. Washington, D.C.: Howard University School of Divinity, 1991.

Perdue, Charles L. Jr., et al., eds. *Weevils in the Wheat: Interviews with Virginia Ex-Slaves*. Bloomington: Indiana University Press, 1980; originally published by the University Press of Virginia in 1976.

Pero, Albert and Ambrose Mayo, eds. *Theology and the Black Experience*. Minneapolis: Augsburg Press, 1988.

Perry, Bruce. ed. *Malcolm X: The Last Speeches*. New York: Pathfinder Press, 1989.

_____. *Malcolm: The Life of a Man Who Changed Black America*. Barrytown: Station Hill, 1991.

_____. *Two Speeches by Malcolm X*, 3rd ed. New York: Pathfinder Press, 1990.

Pontifical Commission on Peace and Justice, *The Church and Racism*. Washington, D.C.: United States Catholic Conference, 1990.

Posey, Thaddeus, ed. *Theology: A Portrait in Black*, Proceedings of the Black Catholic Theological Symposium, #1, 1978. Pittsburgh: National Black Catholic Clergy Caucus, 1980.

Raboteau, Albert J. *Slave Religion: The "Invisible" Institution in the Antebellum South*. New York: Oxford University Press, 1978.

_____. *A Fire in the Bones: Reflections on African American Religious History*. Boston: Beacon Press, 1995.

Redkey, Edwin S. *Respect Black: The Writings and Teachings of Henry McNeale Turner*. New York: Seabury, 1971.

Report of the National Advisory Commission on Civil Disorders. New York: Bantam Books, 1968.

Riggs, Marcia. *Awake, Arise and Act: A Womanist Call for Black Liberation*. Cleveland: The Pilgrim Press, 1995.

Rivers, Clarence Joseph. *The Spirit in Worship*. Cincinnati: Stimuli, Inc., 1978.

_____. *This Far by Faith: American Black Worship and Its African Roots*. Cincinnati: Stimuli, Inc., 1977.

Roberts, J. Deotis. *The Prophethood of Black Believers: An African American Political Theology for Ministry*. Maryknoll: Orbis Books, 1995.

_____. *Liberation and Reconciliation: A Black Theology.* Philadelphia: Westminster Press, 1971; republished, rev. ed., Maryknoll: Orbis, 1994.

_____. *Black Theology in Dialogue.* Philadelphia: Westminster Press, 1987.

_____. *Black Theology Today.* New York: Edwin Mellen Press, 1984.

_____. *A Black Political Theology.* Philadelphia: Westminster Press, 1974.

Salley, Columbus and Ronald Behm. *What Color Is Your God? Black Consciousness and the Christian Faith.* Secaucus: Citadel Press, 1988.

Sanders, Cheryl J., ed. *Living the Intersection: Womanism and Afrocentrism in Theology.* Minneapolis: Fortress, 1994.

_____. *Empowerment Ethics for a Liberated People: A Path to African-American Social Transformation.* Minneapolis: Fortress Press, 1995.

Sawyer, Mary, *Black Ecumenism: Implementing the Demands of Justice.* Valley Forge: Trinity Press International, 1994.

Schineller, Peter. *Handbook on Inculturation.* Mahwah: Paulist Press, 1980.

Secretariat for the Liturgy and Secretariat for Black Catholics, National Conference of Catholic Bishops, *Plenty Good Room: The Spirit and Truth of African American Catholic Worship.* Washington, D.C.: USCC Office for Publishing and Promotion Services, 1991.

Sernett, Milton C. *Black Religion and American Evangelicalism: White Protestants, Plantation Missions and the Flowering of Negro Christianity 1787-1865,* ATLA Monograph Series, No. 7. Metuchen: Scarecrow Press and the American Theological Library Association, 1975.

Smith, Timothy L. "Slavery and Theology: The Emergence of Black Christian Consciousness in Nineteenth Century America" in *Church History* 41, 1972.

Southern, Eileen. *The Music of Black America.* New York: Norton, 2nd ed., 1983.

Spencer, Jon. *Sing a New Song: Liberating Black Hymnody.* Minneapolis: Fortress Press, 1995.

_____. *The Rhythms of Black Folk*. N.Y.: African World Press, 1995.

_____. *Black Hymnody*. Knoxville: University of Tennessee Press, 1992.

_____. *Protest and Praise: Sacred Music of Black Religion*. Minneapolis: Fortress Press, 1990.

Stewart, Carlyle Fielding III. *African American Church Growth*. Nashville: Abingdon Press, 1995.

Thislethwaite, Susan Brooks. *Sex, Race and God: Christian Feminism in Black and White*. New York: Crossroad, 1989.

Thurman, Howard. *Jesus and the Disinherited*. Richmond: Friends Press, 1981; originally published by Abingdon Press in 1949.

Tillich, Paul. *Dynamics of Faith*. New York: Harper and Row, 1957.

Townes, Emilie. *A Troubling in My Soul: Womanist Perspectives on Evil and Suffering*. Maryknoll: Orbis Books, 1994.

_____. *In a Blaze of Glory: Womanist Spirituality as Social Witness*. Nashville: Abingdon Press, 1995.

_____. *Womanist Justice, Womanist Hope*. Atlanta: Scholars Press, 1994.

Truth, Sojourner. "Address to the Ohio Women's Rights Convention," 1851.

United States Catholic Conference, *Brothers and Sisters to Us: U.S. Bishops' Pastoral Letter on Racism in Our Day*. Washington, D.C.: USCC, 1979.

U.S. Catholic Historian, vols. 5, 1986 and 7, 1988. (Special issues on the history of Black Catholics and the National Black Catholic Congress in 1987)

Van den Hengel, John W. *The Home of Meaning: The Hermeneutic of the Subject of Paul Ricouer*. Washington, D.C.: University Press of America 1982.

Walker, Alice. *In Search of Our Mothers' Gardens: Womanist Prose*. New York: Harcourt Brace Jovanovich, 1983.

Walker, David. "Appeal in Four Articles," in Mullane, op. cit.

Washington , Booker T. "The Atlanta Exposition Address," 1895 in Mullane, op. cit.

_____. *Up from Slavery*. New York: Penguin, 1986; first published 1901.

Washington, James Melvin. *Conversations with God: Two Centuries of Prayers by African Americans*. New York: HarperCollins, 1994.

Washington, Joseph R. *The Politics of God*. Boston: Beacon Press, 1967.

_____. *Black Religion: The Negro and Christianity in the United States*. Boston: Beacon Press, 1964.

Washington, Mary Helen. *Invented Lives: Narratives of Black Women, 1860-1960*. Garden City: Doubleday, 1978.

Weems, Renita. *Just a Sister Away: A Womanist Vision of Women's Relationships in the Bible*. San Diego: LuraMedia, 1988.

_____. *I Asked for Intimacy*. San Diego: LuraMedia, 1993.

_____. *Battered Love: Marriage, Sex and Violence in the Hebrew Prophets*. Minneapolis: Fortress Press, 1995.

Weisenberger, Bernard A. *They Gathered at the River: The Story of the Great Revivalists and Their Impact Upon Religion in America*. Chicago: Quadrangle Books, 1966.

West, Cornel. *Prophesy Deliverance! An Afro-American Revolutionary Christianity*. Philadelphia: The Westminster Press, 1986.

_____. *Prophetic Fragments*. Grand Rapids: Eerdmans, 1988.

_____. *Beyond Eurocentrism and Multiculturalism*, vol. 1, *Prophetic Thought in Post-Modern Time;* vol. 2, *Prophetic Reflections: Notes on Race and Power in America*. Monroe: Common Courage Press, 1993.

_____. *Race Matters*. Boston: Beacon Press, 1993.

_____. *Keeping Faith: Philosophy and Race in America*. New York: Routledge, 1993.

Wilentz, Gay. *Binding Cultures: Black Women Writers in Africa and the Diaspora*. Bloomington, Indiana University Press, 1992.

Williams, Dolores. "Womanist Theology: Black Women's Voices" in *Christianity and Crisis*, March 2, 1987.

_____. *Sisters in the Wilderness*. Maryknoll: Orbis, 1993.

Williams, Patricia J. *The Alchemy of Race and Rights*. Cambridge: Harvard University Press, 1991.

Wilmore, Gayraud S. and James H. Cone, eds. *Black Theology: A Documentary History, 1966-1979*. Maryknoll: Orbis, 1979.

_____. *Black Religion and Black Radicalism*. Garden City: Doubleday and Co., 1972; 2nd edition, 1983, Orbis Books.

Wood, Forrest G. *The Arrogance of Faith: Christianity and Race in America from the Colonial Era to the Twentieth Century*. Boston: Northeastern University Press, 1990.

Woodson, Carter. *The Education of the Negro*, republished Brooklyn: A & B Books, 1992.

_____. *The Miseducation of the Negro*. republished Brooklyn: A & B Books, 1992.

Woodward, C. Vann. *The Strange Career of Jim Crow*. New York: Oxford University Press, 1955; 3rd rev. ed., 1974.

Yetman, Norman R. *Life Under the "Peculiar Institution": Selections from the Slave Narrative Collection*. New York: Holt, Rinehart and Winston, 1970.,

Young, Josiah. *Black and African Theologies: Siblings or Distant Cousins?* Maryknoll: Orbis Books, 1986.

Index